Juz' 'Amma: 30

For The Classroom

Larsa Ahmed

PART 30 OF THE HOLY QUR'ĀN

(With Al-Fātiḥah)

Junior Level

Volume 1

From An-Nās 114 to Sūrah Ash-Shams 91

Arabic Text, Transliteration, Translations, and Explanation

Revised Translations

'Abdullāh Yūsuf 'Ali & Moḥammad Marmaduke Pickthall

Compilation By

Abidullah Ghazi

IQRA'

International Educational Foundation

Part of a Comprehensive and Systematic Program of Islamic Studies

A Textbook for
Qur'anic Studies
Junior Level/General

Juz' 'Amma: 30, Vol. I
for the Classroom

Chief Program Editors
Dr. Abidullah al-Ansari Ghazi
(Ph.D. History of Religion,
Harvard University)

Dr. Tasneema Ghazi
(Ph.D. Curriculum-Reading,
University of Minnesota)

Reviewed by
Fadel Abdallah
(M.A. Arabic Islamic Studies,
University of Minnesota)

Dr. Khwaja Moinul Hassan
(Ph. D.English, Purdue University)

Maulana Shuaib-ud-Din
(Faḍil, Dar ul-Ulūm Karachi)

Fouad Al-Mimouni
(M.A., English Literature)

Language Editing
Labiba Hassan
(M.A. English, Dhaka University)

Mahlaqa Patel

Suhaib H. Ghazi
(J.D., University of Illionois)

Typesetting
Ammar Ansari (English)
(M.S., University of Illinois, Chicago)

Randa Zaiter (Arabic)
(B.S. Social Science,
University of Lebanon)

Cover Design
Jennifer Mazzoni
(B.A. Illustration,
Columbia College Chicago)

Acknowledgments:

Dr. Majid Qureshi, M.D. and his wife, Mrs. Farhat Qureshi, of Cincinnati for their encouragement and support

First Edition 1994
Second Revised Edition 1995
Third Printing August 1997
Fourth Printing June, 1999
Fifth Printing July, 2000
Sixth Printing April, 2001
Seventh Printing September, 2005
Eighth Printing November, 2007
Ninth Printing December, 2009
Tenth Printing December, 2011
Eleventh Printing June, 2012
Printed in USA

LCCN: 95-77846
ISBN # 1-56316-109-5

Table of Contents

بِسْمِ اللَّهِ الرَّحْمَٰنِ الرَّحِيمِ

JUZ' 'AMMA: 30

IQRA'S NOTE: To Parents and Teachers

IQRA' International is pleased to offer two textbooks at the junior level: ***Juz' 'Amma*[1]*: 30, Volume 1 (From An-Nās:114 to Ash-Shams: 89 with Sūrah Al-Fātiḥah: 1) and Juz''Amma:30, Volume 2 (From Al-Balad:90 to An-Naba':78).*** The order of the *Suwar*, in these textbooks, is reversed to facilitate the reading , memorization and understanding of the shorter *Suwar* before the longer *Suwar*.

Most of the *Suwar* in the last *Juz'* (30) are Makkan and deal with the theme of *Tawḥīd* (The Oneness of Allāh), *The Risālah* (Prophethood), *Al-'Ākhirah,* (the Hereafter), establishment of the *Qiyāmah,* (The Day of Judgment), the pleasure of *Jannah* and the ordeals of *Jahannam.* These enjoin virtues such as faith, patience, perseverance, trust, hope, generosity and honesty. These encourage social justice, care for the relatives, poor and needy, concern for neighbors, fair dealings, respect for life, freedom of worship, religious tolerance and hospitality. These condemn disbelief, debauchery, falsehood, scandals, miserliness, oppression and arrogance. These were the teachings of the Qur'ān which, under the guidance of the Prophet (S), inspired the Makkans and early converts, brought them into the fold of Islam and prepared them for the greatest sacrifices.

These two textbooks with accompanying workbooks provide, for both an interested reader and a teacher of Qur'ānic Studies, the opportunity to understand the basic teachings of the Qur'ān on some key concepts as presented, so powerfully and graphically, in the early Makkan *Suwar.* Two other textbooks on Qurānic theme, *The Message of the Qur'ān, Volumes: I and II,* a thematic study of the meaning and the message of the Qur'ān , are in progress and we hope to publish them by Fall 1995, *'Inshā' Allāh.*

The teachers may be aware of our earlier publications, *Short Sūrahs* and *Teachings of the Qur'ān*: *Volume 1* (now Volumes I, II, III and IV are available), written as textbooks at elementary level which have been received with great enthusiasm in the class-rooms. These textbooks represented the first attempt to systematically introduce the Message of the Qur'ān to our children at their level of comprehension.

This textbook is a part of IQRA'*s Comprehensive and Systematic Program of Islamic Studies* which encompasses four levels: *Pre-School, Elementary, Junior* and *Senior* and covers ten subjects.

---

1. In the two volumes of *Juz''Amma: 30* the order of the Sūrahs is in the reverse order to facilitate the reading, understanding and memorization for student.

Division of the Juz': Juz''Amma has been divided into two volumes; the first contains 26 *lessons* covering twenty-five (25) *Suwar* and the second volume contains 24 *lessons* covering 13 *Suwar.* Each *Sūrah* starts with an introduction, its title in Arabic, *Sūrah* number and the number of the *'Āyāt.* Each short *Sūrah* is treated as one complete lesson, while the longer *Suwar* are divided into two or more lessons. When the long *Sūrah* is divided into two lessons the introduction is not repeated.

Lesson Plan: Each lesson contains ***Introduction, Arabic text, transliteration, translations*** ('Abdullāh Yūsuf 'Ali and M. M. Pickthal), ***explanation, We Have Learned, and a complete vocabulary of Arabic text***; each part of the lesson plan needs some further explanation.

Transliteration: In transliteration we follow the Library of Congress System with few modifications (See Appendix I). We have followed phonetic method to facilitate the reading. The Arabic definite article *(al)* often assimilates its initial (a) in speech while in writing it does appear. Following the phonetic scheme we have not written it in transliteration. A letter appearing in the text but falling silent after the *'Āyah* is shown in the vocabulary within parenthesis. In transliterating the *Sūrah* we have followed only phonetic sound (as it must be pronounced before the *'Āyah*). The *ḥarakat* (*i'rāb*) do appear on the last letter of the *'Āyah* but they are not read. We have put the silent *ḥarakāt* in parenthesis. For example:

1:1. *Rabbi al-'ālamīna* is written as *Rabbi-(a)l-'ālamīn(a)*
114:1. *Bi-Rabbi an-nāsi* is written as *Bi-Rabbi-(a)n-nās(i)*
Fi Al-Qur'āni al-Karīmi is transliterated as *fi-(a)l-Qur'āni-(a)l-Karīm(i);*

We have followed the phonetic rule in the usage of *Shamsi* (sun) letters for example:

1:1 *Al-Raḥmāni Al-Raḥīmi* is transliterated as *Ar-Raḥmāni-(a)r-Raḥīm(i).*
114:1 *'Ilāhi al-nās* is transliterated as *'Ilāhi-(a)n-nās*

The *Sūrah* is written in Arabic and transliterated in English to help facilitate the readers' pronunciation in case he/she has not yet learned to read Arabic script. However, it is the policy of IQRA' not to encourage this practice and the entire program of IQRA' is designed to teach the students reading and understanding of Qur'ānic Arabic. We shall soon publish another edition of this textbook without transliteration for those who want to develop Arabic reading skills without depending on transliteration.

Translation: We have provided **two major translations of 'Abdullāh Yūsuf 'Ali** (the first translation) and **Muhammad Marmaduke Pickthal** (the second translation) side by side. A student would greatly benifit by the understanding of the Qur'ān from these two prominent scholars, he/she will also understand the difficulties of translating a text like the Qur'ān.

We have taken the liberty to modestly revise the two versions by changing their Biblical language into modern usage without tampering with the text at all. We have also used more accepted Islamic terminology (Allāh for God, Messenger for Apostle).

Commentary: We have used traditional authentic sources to give accepted version of the verses. We have, however, kept the comments to the minimum and allowed the text to speak for itself.

We Have Learned: deals with the central message of the *Sūrah* and reinforces what has been learned.

Vocabulary: The transliteration and the meaning of each word is provided for every *Sūrah* at the end of each lesson. The repitition of the word and careful selection of vocabulary will greatly enhance student's understanding of the Qur'ānic text and will facilitate him/ her in learning Arabic.

Workbooks based on the pattern of our completed and familiar *Sīrah Program* are under publication to provide for reinforcement, develop educational skills and provide further practice.

This work is a major effort to introduce the meaning and message of the Qur'ān at every level and we pray to Allāh (SWT) to accept this effort and make it useful to all the lovers of the truth as contained in the Holiest Book and the Purest of the Messages.

As a concerned parent and teacher, we urge you to support this pioneering educational effort through your *Du'ā'*, advice and financial contributions. IQRA' International invites you to participate in our educational vision by:

a) Becoming Anṣārs of Iqra' Educational Program,
b) Enrolling as members of Iqra' Book Club.

We shall appreciate your opinion and comments to help us improve the revised edition.

Note on Second Revised Edition: *Al-ḥamdu li-(A)llāh,* we are presenting this Second Revised Edition. The First Edition was very warmly received by our readers, and ran out soon after publication. This edition incorporates many useful suggestions by teachers and readers to improve this work. May Allāh reward them for their work and cooperation.

Chief Editors
7450 Skokie Blvd.
Skokie, IL 60077

Monday, February 27, 1995
27 Ramaḍānu-(a)l-Mubārak 1415

سورة الفاتحة ١

Lesson 1

AL-FĀTIHAH, 1:1-7

THE OPENING CHAPTER / THE OPENING

Revealed in Makkah

INTRODUCTION:

Sūrah al-Fātihah is the first *Sūrah* of the Qur'ān. It is regarded as the greatest *Sūrah* of the Qur'ān. It is also known by many other names, the most famous of which is *'Ummu-(a)l-Kitāb,* the "Mother of the Book." Its relation to the whole Qur'ān is like that of a mother to a child.

Rasūlullāh (S) said of this *Sūrah:*

"Such an important *Sūrah* as this was not sent down to any other prophet."

Sūrah al-Fātihah is a prayer taught to us by Allāh (SWT) and He promises to accept the prayers made in this *Sūrah.* It is recited in the beginning of each *rak'ah,* during daily *salāh.*

TRANSLITERATION:	**ARABIC TEXT:**
1. *Bismillāhi-(a)r-Rāḥmāni-(a)r-Raḥīm(i)*	بسم الله الرحمن الرحيم -
2. *Al-ḥamdu li-(A)llāhi Rabbi-(a)l-'ālamīn(a)*	الحمد لله رب العلمين -۝
3. *Ar-Raḥmāni-(a)r-Raḥīm(i)*	الرحمن الرحيم -۝
4. *Māliki yawmi-(a)d-dīn(i)*	ملك يوم الدين -۝
5. *'Iyyā-ka na'budu wa 'iyyā-ka nasta'īn(u)*	إياك نعبد وإياك نستعين -۝
6. *'Ihdina-(a)ṣ-ṣirāt al-mustaqīm(a)*	اهدنا الصراط المستقيم -۝
7. *Ṣirāta-(a)l-ladhīna an'amta 'alai-him*	صراط الذين أنعمت عليهم غير -
Ghairi-(a)l-maghḍūbi 'alai-him wa la-(a)ḍ-ḍāallīn(a)	المغضوب عليهم ولا الضالين ۝

TRANSLATIONS:[2]

By Abdullah Yusuf Ali

1. In the name of Allāh, Most-Gracious, Most Merciful.
2. Praise be to Allāh The Cherisher and Sustainer of the Worlds;
3. Most Gracious, Most Merciful;
4. Master of the Day of Judgment.
5. You do we worship, and Your aid we seek.
6. Show us the straight way,
7. The way of those on whom You have bestowed Your Grace, those whose (portion) is not wrath, and who go not astray.

By Muhammad Marmaduke Pickthal

1. In the name of Allāh, the Beneficent, the Merciful
2. Praise be to Allāh, Lord of the Worlds:
3. The Beneficent, the Merciful:
4. Owner of the Day of Judgment.
5. You alone we worship; You (alone) we ask for help.
6. Show us the straight path:
7. The path of those whom You have favored; Not (the path) of those who earn Your anger nor of those who go astray.

EXPLANATION:

1. The verse *Bismillāhi-(a)r-Raḥmāni-(a)r-Raḥīm* marks the beginning of every *Sūrah* in the Qur'ān, with the exception of *Sūrah at-Tawbah.* This *'āyah* mentions two of the most beautiful names of Allāh (SWT), *Ar-Raḥmān* and *Ar-Raḥīm. Ar-Raḥmān* means Mercy-Giving. *Ar-Raḥīm* means very Merciful. Both these names of Allāh (SWT) emphasize His infinite Kindness and Mercy.

2. All praises belong to Allāh (SWT) alone. He is the Lord, Creator and Sustainer of all the worlds. He, alone, has given us all that we have. Allāh (SWT), alone, is perfect. He is our Creator and our Sustainer. He knows what is best for us. We should understand that all that happens is part of Allāh's plan and has a specific purpose behind it. We should praise Him in all things.

3. Allāh (SWT) is the Most-Kind and Most-Merciful. If we commit a sin, or make a mistake, and repent, He forgives us. He rewards us for all our good actions many times over.

4. Allāh (SWT), alone, is the Master of the Day of Judgment. None will share His power on that Day. He will reward the Righteous with *Jannah,* and punish the evil-doers with *Jahannam.*

---

2. Two popular translations are given side by side in this textbook: the first is by `Abdullāh Yūsuf `Ali and the second is by Muḥammad Marmaduke Pickthal. We hope that the readers will find this comparative reading both educational and informative.

5. As Muslims, we worship only Allāh (SWT). We cannot worship idols, stones, trees, rivers, stars, angels, or any other power besides Allāh (SWT). Muslims seek help only from Allāh (SWT). No one may help us if Allāh (SWT) does not wish it. If any help is given to us, it is with the permission of Allāh (SWT). Therefore, we must seek only Allāh's (SWT) help.

6. We ask Him to guide us on the straight path of Islam. Allāh (SWT) commands us to follow this religion alone. Those who had followed the path of Islam in the past were rewarded by Allāh (SWT).

7. We must follow the path of Islam, because Allāh (SWT) rewards those who do so. This religion had been followed by the prophets, the martyrs, the truthful and the righteous. We must strive to follow the path of those who have been favored by Allāh (SWT). We should not follow the path of those with whom Allāh (SWT) is angry, the path of *Shaiṭān.* Allāh (SWT) punishes those who follow this evil path. We seek refuge from Allāh's anger.

WE HAVE LEARNED:

* Allāh (SWT) is our Lord and Creator.
* We must worship Him, alone, and turn to Him for all our needs.
* We ask Allāh (SWT) the path of those who were guided to the right path.

VOCABULARY

اَلتَّعَوُّذُ

﴿ أَعُوذُ بِٱللَّهِ مِنَ ٱلشَّيْطَٰنِ ٱلرَّجِيمِ ﴾

Word الكلمة	Transliteration لفظها	Meaning معناها
أَعُوذُ	*'A'ūdhu*	I seek refuge
بِ	*bi*	in, with
اَللّٰهِ	*'Allāh(i)*	God
مِنْ	*min*	from
اَلشَّيْطٰنِ	*Ash-Shaiṭān(i)*	the Devil
اَلرَّجِيْمِ	*Ar-Rajīm(i)*	the accursed

VOCABULARY

١-سورة الفاتحة

١-بِسْمِ اللَّهِ	*Bismillāh(i)*	In the Name of Allah
الرَّحْمَـٰنِ	*'ar-Raḥmān(i)*	The Most Gracious, The Beneficent
الرَّحِيْمِ	*'ar-Raḥīm(i)*	the Most Merciful
٢-اَلْ	*Al*	the, definite article
حَمْدُ	*ḥamdu*	praise
لِلَّهِ	*Li-(A)llāh(i)*	for, due to
رَبِّ	*Rabb*	Lord, Allah
الْعَالَمِيْنَ	*al-'ālamīn(a)*	(of) the worlds
٣- الرَّحْمٰنِ	*Ar-Raḥmān(i)*	The Most Gracious, The Beneficent
الرَّحِيْمِ	*Ar-Raḥīm(i)*	The Most Kind
٤-مَٰلِكِ	*Mālik(i)*	Master, Owner
يَومِ	*Yawm(i)*	Day (of)
اَلدِّيْنِ	*Ad-Dīn(i)*	The Judgment
٥-إِيَّاكَ	*'Iyyā-ka*	(to) You alone, only to You
نَعْبُدُ	*na'bud(u)*	We worship
وَ	*wa*	and
إِيَّاكَ	*'iyyā-ka*	(from) you alone
نَسْتَعِيْنُ	*nasta'īn(u)*	we seek aid, help
٦-إِهْدِنَا	*' Ihdi-n(a)*	Show us, guide us
اَلصِّرَاطَ	*aṣ-ṣiraṭ*	the way, the path

اَلْمُسْتَقِيْمَ	*al-mustaqīm(a)*	the straight, smooth
٧-صِراطَ	*Ṣirāt(a)*	way, path (of)
اَلذَّيِنَ	*'alladhīna*	those, who
أنْعَمْتَ	*'an'amta*	you bestowed grace, you favored
عَلَىٰ	*'alā*	on, upon
هِمْ	*him*	them
غَيْرِ	*ghair(i)*	not of those
اَلْمَغْضُوبِ	*al-maghḍūb(i)*	earned the anger
عَلَيْهِمْ	*'alai-him*	on them
وَ	*wa*	and
لاَ	*la*	not, neither
اَلضَّالِّيْنَ	*'aḍ-ḍāallin(a)*	who went astray, went off the path

سُورَةُ النَّاسِ

Lesson 2

AN-NĀS, 114:1-6

MANKIND / MANKIND

Revealed in Makkah

INTRODUCTION:

There are 114 *Suwar* (plural of *Sūrah*), in the Qur'ān. *Sūrah* an-Nās is the last *Sūrah* of the Qur'ān. This is a twin *Sūrah* with *Sūrah al-Falaq*, or "The Daybreak."

In both these *Suwar*, we seek refuge in Allāh (SWT) from all forms of evils and dangers. In this *Sūrah*, we seek Allāh's refuge from the evil that come from inside us.

Rasūlullāh (S) advised us to recite these two *Suwar* in the morning and at night, before we go to sleep. If we do so, Allāh (SWT) promises to save us from the evil and danger that comes from inside us or that which is around us.

TRANSLITERATION:	**ARABIC TEXT:**
Bismillāhi-(a)r-Raḥmāni-(a)r-Raḥīm(i)	بِسْمِ اللَّهِ الرَّحْمَٰنِ الرَّحِيمِ
1. *Qul 'a'ūdhu bi-Rabbi-(a)n-nās(i)*	قُلْ أَعُوذُ بِرَبِّ النَّاسِ ۝
2. *Maliki-(a)n-nās(i)*	مَلِكِ النَّاسِ ۝
3. *'Ilāhi-(a)n-nās(i)*	إِلَٰهِ النَّاسِ ۝
4. *Min sharri-(a)l-waswāsi-(a)l-khannās(i)*	مِن شَرِّ الْوَسْوَاسِ الْخَنَّاسِ ۝
5. *'Alladhī yuwaswisu fī ṣudūri-(a)n-nās(i)*	الَّذِي يُوَسْوِسُ فِي صُدُورِ النَّاسِ ۝
6. *Mina-(a)l-jinnati wa-(a)n-nās(i)*	مِنَ الْجِنَّةِ وَالنَّاسِ ۝

TRANSLATIONS:

In the name of Allāh, Most Gracious, Most Merciful.

1. Say: I seek refuge with the Lord and Cherisher of Mankind,
2. The King (or Ruler) of Mankind,
3. The God (or Judge) of Mankind,
4. From the mischief of the Whisperer (of evil), who withdraws (after his whisper),
5. (The same) who whispers into the hearts of Mankind,
6. Among Jinns and among Men.

In the name of Allāh, the Beneficent, the Merciful.

1. Say: I seek refuge in the Lord of mankind,
2. The King of mankind,
3. The God of mankind,
4. From the evil of the sneaking whisperer
5. Who whispers in the hearts of mankind,
6. Of the jinn and of mankind.

EXPLANATION:

114:1. As Muslims, we know that Allāh (SWT) has power over everything. No one else shares this power with Him.. No one may help us or harm us without Allāh's permission. Therefore we always ask Allāh's protection and refuge from all evil forces that are within us or around us.

114:2. Allāh (SWT) is the King and Ruler of all the worlds. No one shares power with Him (SWT).

114:3. Allāh (SWT) is the only God for all of mankind. He is the God of those who believe in Him. He is also the God of those who do not believe in Him. There is no God except Allāh (SWT).

114:4. We seek Allāh's protection from the *Shaiṭān*, who places evil thoughts into the hearts of people. Many people do not realize that these thoughts are from the *Shaiṭān.* He is the worst enemy of mankind. When we follow the Qur'ān and the *Sunnah* of Rasūlullāh (S), the *Shaiṭān* avoids us.

114:5-6. Among men and *jinn* are those who behave as the *Shaiṭān* does. They are evil, and they place evil thoughts into the minds of people. The best way to prevent this from happening to us is to avoid the company of such evil people. Instead, we should seek the company of better people. And we must always trust Allāh's powers and seek His protection. One who is protected by Allāh (SWT) cannot be harmed by anyone.

WE HAVE LEARNED:

* Allāh is the Lord of everyone.
* We must seek His protection from the evil inspired by *Shaiṭān.*
* *Shayāṭīn* exist both among *Jinns* and among humans.

VOCABULARY

١١٤-سُورَةُ النَّاسِ

١-قُلْ	*Qul*	Say
أَعُوذُ	*'a'ūdhu*	I seek refuge
بِ	*bi*	In, with
رَبِّ	*Rabb(i)*	King, Ruler, Lord
اَلنَّاسِ	*an-nās(i)*	mankind, the people
٢-مَلِكِ	*Malik(i)*	King, Ruler
اَلنَّاسِ	*'an-nās(i)*	mankind, people
٣-إِلَٰهِ	*' Ilāh(i)*	The God, the Judge
اَلنَّاسِ	*'an-nās(i)*	humankind, people
٤-مِنْ	*Min*	From
شَرِّ	*sharr(i)*	(the) mischief, evil (of)
اَلْوَسْوَاسِ	*'al-waswās(i)*	the whisperer, the *Shaiṭān*
اَلْخَنَّاسِ	*'al-khannās(i)*	one who withdraws, the sneaky
٥-اَلَّذِى	*'Alladhī*	one who, who
يُوَسْوِسُ	*yuwaswisu*	whispers, puts evil ideas
فِي صُدُورِ	*fi ṣudūr(i)*	in (the) hearts, chests (of)
اَلنَّاسِ	*'an-nās(i)*	the humankind, people
٦-مِنَ	*Min(a)*	From, among, of
اَلْجِنَّةِ	*al-jinnat(i)*	the jinns
وَ	*wa*	and
اَلنَّاسِ	*'an-nās(i)*	The humankind, people

سُوْرَةُ الْفَلَقِ

Lesson 3

AL-FALAQ, 113:1-5

THE DAYBREAK / THE DAYBREAK

Revealed in Makkah

INTRODUCTION:

This is the twin *Sūrah* to *Sūrah 'an-Nās*. In this *Sūrah*, we seek refuge in Allāh (SWT) from the evils that come from outside of us.

We ask Allāh (SWT) to save us from the evil of witchcraft, and from the jealousy of the jealous people.

TRANSLITERATION:	**ARABIC TEXT:**
Bismillāhi-(a)r-Raḥmāni-(a)r-Raḥīm(i)	بِسْمِ اللّٰهِ الرَّحْمٰنِ الرَّحِيْمِ
1. *Qul 'a'ūdhu bi-Rabbi-(a)l-falaq(i)*	قُلْ اَعُوْذُ بِرَبِّ الْفَلَقِ ۝
2. *Min sharri mā Khalaq(a)*	مِنْ شَرِّ مَا خَلَقَ ۝
3. *Wa min sharri ghāsiqin 'idhā waqab(a)*	وَمِنْ شَرِّ غَاسِقٍ اِذَا وَقَبَ ۝
4. *Wa min sharrri-(a)n-naffāthāti fi-(a)l-'uqad(i)*	وَمِنْ شَرِّ النَّفّٰثٰتِ فِى الْعُقَدِ ۝
5. *Wa min sharri ḥāsidin 'idhā ḥasad(a)*	وَمِنْ شَرِّ حَاسِدٍ اِذَا حَسَدَ ۝

TRANSLATIONS:

In the name of Allāh, Most Gracious, Most Merciful.

1. Say; I seek refuge with the Lord of the Dawn,
2. From the mischief of created things;

In the name of Allāh, the Beneficent, the Merciful.

1. Say: I seek refuge in the Lord of Daybreak.
2. From the evil of that which He created;

3. And from the mischief of Darkness as it over spreads;	3. And from the evil of the darkness when it is intense,
4. From the mischief of those who practice Secret Arts.	4. And from the evil of malignant witchcraft,
5. And from the mischief of the envious one as he practices envy.	5. And from the evil of the envier when he envieth.

EXPLANATION:

113:1. Allāh (SWT) is the Lord and Creator of all things. He has created the darkness and the light. He brings light out of darkness. He shows us the light of Islam and saves us from the darkness of disbelief.

113:2. Everything has been created by Allāh (SWT). Some things are beneficial, while other things may harm us. All power belongs to Allāh (SWT) and He, alone, may protect us from the harmful things that He has created. He, alone, has the power to make the things He has created beneficial for us.

113:3. We seek refuge in Allāh (SWT) from the evils that are contained within the darkness of the night. Many evil and forbidden things occur in the cover of the night.

113:4. Witchcraft is forbidden in Islam. It should not be practiced under any circumstances. Some ignorant people of ancient Arabia would practice witchcraft by blowing on the knots of a string but there are many other forms of magic as well.

113:5. Jealousy is a very bad thing. A person who displays jealousy never does any good to himself, yet he feels jealous of those who have been more blessed by Allāh (SWT). A jealous person always tries to destroy others. May Allāh (SWT) protect us from the jealousy of others and keep our hearts pure from jealousy as well.

WE HAVE LEARNED:

* *Al-Falaq* is the twin *Sūrah* with *An-Nās*.
* In this we seek Allāh's refuge from the evils which come from outside.
* We seek His protection from the evil of all the things that He has created.

VOCABULARY

١١٣-سُورَةُ الفَلَق

١-قُلْ	*Qul*	Say
أعُوذُ	*'a'ūdhu*	I seek refuge
بِرَبِّ	*bi-Rabb(i)*	with, in the Lord, the Cherisher (of)
اَلْفَلَقِ	*'al-falaq(i)*	Day-break
٢-مِنْ	*Min*	From
شَرِّ	*sharr(i)*	the mischief, evil
مَا	*mā*	which, of,what, what thing
خَلَقَ	*khalaq(a)*	He created
٣-وَمِنْ	*Wa-min*	And from
شَرِّ	*sharr(i)*	the mischief, evil
غَاسِقٍ	*ghāsiq(in)*	darkness
إِذَا	*'idhā*	when
وَقَبَ	*waqab(a)*	spreads, comes on
٥-وَمِنْ	*Wa-min*	And from
شَرِّ	*sharr(i)*	the mischief, evil
اَلنَّفّٰثٰتِ	*an-naffāthāt(i)*	The blower in or on something
فِى اَلْعُقَدِ	*fi -l- `uqad(i)*	in the knots
٦-وَمِنْ	*Wa-min*	And from
شَرِّ	*Sharr(i)*	the mischief, evil
حَاسِدٍ	*ḥāsid(in)*	envious person, jealous person
إِذَا حَسَدَ	*'idhā ḥasad(a)*	when he envies, he practices jealousy

Lesson 4

AL-'IKHLĀṢ, 112:1-4

PURITY (OF FAITH) / THE SINCERITY

Revealed in Makkah

INTRODUCTION:

This short *Sūrah* is one of the most important *Suwar* in the Qur'ān. This *Sūrah* teaches us about *Tawḥīd*, or "Oneness of Allāh." The central theme of the Qur'ān is *Tawḥīd*, the Oneness of Allāh. Rasūlullāh (S) described this *Sūrah* as being equal to one third of the Qur'ān: about one-third of the Qur'ān deals with the meaning and message of *Tawhīd*. *Al-'Ikhlāṣ* means "Sincerity." Allāh (SWT) wants us to have complete, sincere faith in *Tawḥīd*..

TRANSLITERATION:	**ARABIC TEXT:**
Bismillāhi-(a)r-Raḥmāni-(a)r-Raḥīm(i)	بِسْمِ اللّٰهِ الرَّحْمٰنِ الرَّحِيْمِ
1. *Qul huwa-(A)llāhu 'aḥad(un)*	-قُلْ هُوَ اللّٰهُ اَحَدٌ ۝
2. *Allāhu-(a)ṣ-Ṣamad(u)*	-اَللّٰهُ الصَّمَدُ ۝
3. *Lam yalid wa lam yūlad*	-لَمْ يَلِدْ ۙ وَلَمْ يُوْلَدْ ۝
4. *Wa lam yaku-l lahū kufuwan 'aḥad(un)*	-وَلَمْ يَكُنْ لَّهٗ كُفُوًا اَحَدٌ ۝

TRANSLATIONS:

In the name of Allāh, Most Gracious,
Most Merciful.
1. Say: He is Allāh, the One and Only;
2. Allāh, the Eternal, Absolute;
3. He Begetteth not, nor is He begotten;
4. And there is none like unto Him.

In the name of Allāh, the Beneficent,
the Merciful.
1. Say: He is Allāh, the One!
2. Allāh, the eternally Besought of all!
3. He begets not, nor was He begotten:
4. And there is none comparable unto Him.

EXPLANATION:

112:1. Allāh (SWT) is *Al-'Aḥad*, the One. None can compare unto Him. He has created us, cares for us, and unto Him shall we return. We should worship no one but Allāh (SWT).

112:2. Allāh (SWT) is *Aṣ-Ṣamad*, which means "One who is Eternal." *Aṣ-Ṣamad* is the One on whom everyone depends. *Aṣ-Ṣamad*, Himself, is independent of anyone. He is One who creates everything and watches over everything, and everything returns to Him. He does not need anyone to care for Him.

112:3. Allāh (SWT) is the Creator of all things. No one has created Allāh (SWT) or has given birth to Him. He does not give birth to anyone or anything. Allāh (SWT) is our Lord and Creator and He has the power to create all things by a single command: "Be!" and it is.

112:4. Everything, living or non-living, is a creation of Allāh (SWT). No one shares His power. No one can be compared with Him, and to do so is a sin. To make idols and images of Allāh (SWT) and to worship them is also sinful. Allāh (SWT) is unlike anything that we can ever imagine.

WE HAVE LEARNED:

* Allāh is One.
* He is *Aṣ-Ṣamad*, we all depend upon Him, He does not depend upon anyone or anything.
* He has no partners, sons, daughters or wives.

VOCABULARY

١١٢-سُورَةُ الإِخْلَاص

١-قُلْ	*Qul*	Say
هُوَ ٱللَّهُ	*Huwa-Llāh(u)*	He is Allah
أَحَدٌ	*'Aḥad(un)*	One, Only
٢-اَللَّهُ	*Allāh(u)*	Allah
اَلصَّمَدُ	*Aṣ-Ṣamad(u)*	The Eternal, Absolute
٣-لَمْ يَلِدْ	*Lam yalid*	He begets not, He does not give birth
وَلَمْ يُولَدْ	*wa- lam yūlad*	and He is not begotten, He was not born
٤-وَلَمْ يَكُنْ	*Wa- lam yakun*	And there is not
لَهُ	*la-Hū*	for Him
كُفُوًا	*kufuwan*	equal, comparable
أَحَدٌ	*'aḥad(un)*	Any, anyone

Lesson 5

سُورَةُ المَسَدِ

AL-MASAD / AL-LAHAB, 111:1-5

THE PLAITED ROPE / (THE FATHER OF) FLAME

Revealed in Makkah

INTRODUCTION:

This *Sūrah* speaks about the punishment of 'Abū Lahab and his wife, the two worst enemies of Islam in Makkah during that time. Abū Lahab was the uncle of Rasūlullāh (S) but he was also one of the greatest enemies of Islam. He and his wife strongly opposed him and tried to harm him in every way possible.

Through the story contained in these verses, Allāh (SWT) warns the enemies of Islam that, by trying to hurt the cause of Islam, they actually hurt no one but themselves.

TRANSLITERATION:	ARABIC TEXT:
Bismillāhi-(a)r-Raḥmāni-(a)r-Raḥīm(i)	بِسْمِ اللَّهِ الرَّحْمَٰنِ الرَّحِيمِ
1. *Tabbat yadā 'Abī Lahabin wa-tabb(a)*	١- تَبَّتْ يَدَا أَبِي لَهَبٍ وَتَبَّ ۝
2. *Mā'aghnā 'an-hu mālu-hū wa-mā kasab(a)*	٢- مَا أَغْنَىٰ عَنْهُ مَالُهُ وَمَا كَسَبَ ۝
3. *Sa-yaṣlā nāran dhāta lahab(in)*	٣- سَيَصْلَىٰ نَارًا ذَاتَ لَهَبٍ ۝
4. *Wa-mra'atu-hū ḥammālata-(a)l-ḥaṭab(i)*	٤- وَامْرَأَتُهُ حَمَّالَةَ الْحَطَبِ ۝
5. *Fī- jīdi-hā ḥablum mim-masad(in)*	٥- فِي جِيدِهَا حَبْلٌ مِّن مَّسَدٍ ۝

TRANSLATIONS:

In the name of Allāh, Most Gracious, Most Merciful.

1. Perish the hands of the Father of Flame! Perish he!

In the name of Allāh, the Beneficent, the Merciful.

1. The power of Abū Lahab will perish, and he will perish.

2. No profit to him from all his wealth, and all his gains!
3. Burnt soon will he be in a Fire of blazing Flame!
4. His wife shall carry the (crackling) wood as fuel!
5. A twisted rope of palm-leaf fibre round her (own) neck!

2. His wealth and gains will not exempt him.
3. He will be plunged in flaming fire,
4. And his wife, the wood-carrier,
5. Will have upon her neck a halter of palm-fibre.

EXPLANATION:

111:1. 'Abū Lahab was a very handsome person. His real name was 'Abd al-'Uzzā, "Servant of al-'Uzzā". *Al-'Uzzā* was one of the highest gods of the pagan Arabs. He was also called *'Abū Lahab*, "Father of Flames," because of his reddish skin. The "hands" of 'Abū Lahab refer to the power and influence that he possessed.

111:2. He was a very wealthy and prominent leader of the Quraish. However, all power and wealth belongs to Allāh (SWT). No one may have these things without His permission. In the end, all of 'Abū Lahab's wealth and power could not save him from Allāh's wrath.

111:3. 'Abū Lahab should not have been proud of his red, flame-like face. On the Day of Judgment, he will be thrown in the blazing flames of Hell-fire. His wife will suffer the same fate.

111:4. During the night, his wife would bring thorny firewood and place it in Rasūlullāh's path. Sometimes, he would accidentally walk on the wood and be harmed.

"To carry firewood" also means to tell false tales about people. The wife of 'Abū Lahab used to spread rumors about Rasūlullāh (S), in order to make people turn away from him.

111:5. 'Abū Lahab's wife would tie thorny wood with twisted rope to carry it to Rasūlullāh's home. On the Day of Judgment, her neck will be tied with a twisted rope, made of fire. Like her husband, she will be thrown into a fire of blazing flames.

WE HAVE LEARNED:

* The power of 'Abū Lahab, his wife and the enemies of Islam will fail.
* The trials faced by the believers should be viewed as only tests from Allāh (SWT).
* Ultimately, the Muslims will be triumphant if they remain steadfast in their faith and actions.

VOCABULARY

١١١-سُورَةُ المَسَدِ

١-تَبَّتْ	*Tabbat*	Will perish, perish
يَدَآ	*yadā*	the hands, the two hands (of)
أَبِى لَهَبٍ	*'Abī Lahab(in)*	'Abū Lahab, Father of Flames
وَتَبَّ	*wa tabb(a)*	and (he) will perish
٢-مَآ أَغْنَىٰ	*Mā 'aghnā*	Will not be exempt, will not gain
عَنْهُ	*'an-hu*	to him
مَالُهُ	*mālu-hū*	his wealth
وَمَا	*wa mā*	and what
كَسَبَ	*kasab(a)*	he gained
٣-سَيَصْلَىٰ	*Sa-yaṣlā*	He will be burned
نَارًا	*nāran*	the fire
ذَاتَ	*dhāta*	having, possessing, owning, of
لَهَبٍ	*lahab(in)*	flame, fire with flames
٤-وَٱمْرَأَتُهُ	*Wa-mra' atu-hū*	And his wife, his woman
حَمَّالَةَ	*ḥammālata*	the carrier, (of) the one who carries
اَلْحَطَبِ	*'al-ḥaṭab(i)*	the wood, the firewood
٥-فِى	*Fī*	In
جِيدِهَا	*jīdi-hā*	her neck
حَبْلٌ	*ḥabl(un)*	a rope
مِّنْ	*min*	from, of
مَّسَدٍ	*masad(in)*	fiber of palm leaf

سورة النصر — آياتها ٣ — ترتيبها ١١٠

Lesson 6

AN-NAṢR, 110:1-3

THE HELP / SUCCOUR

Revealed in Madīnah

INTRODUCTION:

An-Naṣr, Victory, was the last complete *Sūrah* to be revealed to Rasūlullāh (S), just before his death. It was revealed after the last *Ḥajj,* called *Ḥijjat ul-Wadā',* the Farewell Pilgrimage; performed by Rasūlullāh (S) in the tenth year of *Ḥijrah.*

In this *Sūrah,* Allāh (SWT) informs Rasūlullāh (S) about the coming victory for Islam, and promises His help in achieving it. This Revelation was also an indication that the mission of Rasūlullāh (S) was now reaching its completion; and thus, he is asked to turn to Allāh (SWT) to seek His forgiveness.

TRANSLITERATION:	ARABIC TEXT:
Bismillāhi-(a)r-Raḥmāni-(a)r-Raḥīm	بِسْمِ اللّٰهِ الرَّحْمٰنِ الرَّحِيْمِ
1. 'Idhā jā'a naṣru-(A)llāhi wa-(a)l-fatḥ(u)	-إِذَا جَآءَ نَصْرُ اللّٰهِ وَالْفَتْحُ ۝
2. Wa ra'ait-an-nāsa yadkhulūna fī dīn-i-(A)llāhi 'afwājā(n)	-وَرَأَيْتَ النَّاسَ يَدْخُلُوْنَ فِيْ دِيْنِ اللّٰهِ أَفْوَاجًا ۝
3. Fa-sabbiḥ bi-ḥamdi Rabbi-ka wa-staghfir-hu inna-hū kāna tawwābā(n)	-فَسَبِّحْ بِحَمْدِ رَبِّكَ وَاسْتَغْفِرْهُ ۚ إِنَّهُ كَانَ تَوَّابًا ۝

TRANSLATIONS:

In the name of Allāh, Most Gracious, Most Merciful.

1. When comes the Help of Allāh and Victory,

In the name of Allāh, the Beneficent, the Merciful.

1. When Allāh's succour and the triumph comes,

2. And you do see the People enter Allāh's Religion in crowds,	2. And you see mankind entering the religion of Allāh in troops,
3. Celebrate the Praises of your Lord and pray for His forgiveness: For He is Oft-Returning (in Grace and Mercy).	3. Then hymn the praises of your Lord and seek forgiveness of Him. Lo! He is ever ready to show mercy.

EXPLANATION:

110:1. Allāh (SWT) has sent Rasūlullāh (S) as His final Messenger and promised him that He would make Islam victorious.

In this *Sūrah*, Allāh (SWT) reveals that the help promised to the Muslims had come and that victory had been achieved. Allāh (SWT) also promises that His help and victory will always be with the Muslims if they keep their faith in Allāh (SWT) and work for the cause of Islam.

110:2. Towards the end of Rasūlullāh's (S) life, many people accepted Islam. They entered the religion in large numbers. By the time of his death, almost all of Arabia had accepted Islam.

110:3. The victory that Islam achieved was due to the efforts of Rasūlūllah (S) and his *Ṣaḥābah*. They were helped by Allāh (SWT). In this *Sūrah*, Rasūlullāh (S) is asked to thank Allāh (SWT) for His help, by glorifying Him and asking His forgiveness.

One of the names of Allāh (SWT) is *Tawwāb*, which means "Oft-Returning". Allāh (SWT) always shows forgiveness and mercy to those who make *Tawbah* (repentance).

WE HAVE LEARNED:

* Allāh (SWT) always keeps His promises to the believers.
* He will always help them achieve victory.
* When the victory of Allāh (SWT) comes, we must turn to Him, glorify Him and ask for His forgiveness.

VOCABULARY

١١٠-سُورَةُ النَّصْر

١-إذا	*'Idhā*	When
جَآءَ	*jā'a*	comes
نَصْرُ ٱللَّهِ	*naṣru-(A)llāh(i)*	the help of Allah, Allah's succor (succour)
وَ	*wa*	and
اَلْفَتْحُ	*'al-fatḥ(u)*	the victory, triumph
٢-ورَأَيْتَ	*Wa-ra'aita*	And you see
اَلنَّاسَ	*'an-nās(a)*	the humankind, people
يَدْخُلُونَ	*yadkhulūna*	(people) entering, enter
فِى	*fī*	In
دِينِ ٱللَّهِ	*dīni-(A)llāh(i)*	the religion of Allah
أَفْوَاجاً	*'afwāj(an)*	(in) crowds, in large numbers
٣-فَسَبِّحْ	*Fa-sabbiḥ*	Then hymn, glorify, recite praises
بِحَمْدِ	*bi-ḥamd-i*	the praising (lit, "with praises")
رَبِّكَ	*Rabbi-ka*	your Lord, your *Rabb*
٣-وَٱسْتَغْفِرْهُ	*Wa-(a)staghfir-hū*	And seek His forgiveness
إِنَّهُ	*'inna-Hū*	for He surely, indeed He
كَانَ	*kāna*	(is) , was
تَوَّابًا	*Tawwāba(an)*	Oft-Returning with Mercy, ever ready to show Mercy (Lit "Oft-Returning with Mercy")

Lesson 7

سُورَةُ الكَافِرُونَ

آياتها ٦ — ترتيبها ١٠٩

AL-KĀFIRŪN, 109:1-6

THOSE WHO REJECT FAITH / THE DISBELIEVERS

Revealed in Makkah

INTRODUCTION:

Islam is the final religion of Allāh (SWT), revealed to Rasūlullāh (S) through Angel Jibrīl (A). Islam is complete as it stands, and no one has the power or the authority to change any part of it. Neither Rasūlullāh (S) nor his *Ṣaḥābah* had the authority to make reductions or additions to the basic message of Islam.

There can never be any compromises made in matters of religion. However, we should not force anyone to practice Islam. Some *Kuffār* wanted an agreement from Rasūlullāh (S). They would agree to worship Allāh (SWT) if the Muslims would worship their idols. Allāh (SWT) rejected the *Kuffār's* offer. In this *Sūrah*, Allāh (SWT) informs Rasūlullāh (S) that there cannot be any form of compromise in religion. On the other hand, there should be no compulsion in religion either.

TRANSLITERATION:	**ARABIC TEXT**:
Bismillāhi-(a)r-Raḥmāni-(a)r-Raḥīm(i)	بِسْمِ اللّٰهِ الرَّحْمٰنِ الرَّحِيمِ
1. *Qul yā 'ayyuha-(a)l-kāfirūn(a)*	قُلْ يٰٓأَيُّهَا الْكٰفِرُونَ ۝ -١
2. *Lā 'a'budu mā ta'budūn(a)*	لَآ أَعْبُدُ مَا تَعْبُدُونَ ۝ -٢
3. *Wa-lā 'antum 'ābidūna mā 'a'bud(u)*	وَلَآ أَنتُمْ عٰبِدُونَ مَآ أَعْبُدُ ۝ -٣
4. *Wa-lā 'anā 'ābidum mā 'abad-tum*	وَلَآ أَنَا عَابِدٌ مَّا عَبَدتُّمْ ۝ -٤
5. *Wa-lā 'antum 'ābidūna mā 'a'bud(u)*	وَلَآ أَنتُمْ عٰبِدُونَ مَآ أَعْبُدُ ۝ -٥
6. *La-kum dīnu-kum wa-li-ya-dīn(i)*	لَكُمْ دِينُكُمْ وَلِىَ دِينِ ۝ -٦

TRANSLATIONS:

In the name of Allāh, Most Gracious,
Most Merciful.

1. Say: O you that reject Faith!
2. I worship not that you worship,
3. Nor will you worship that which I worship.
4. And I will not worship that which you have been wont to worship,
5. Nor will you worship that which I worship.
6. To you be your Way, and to me mine.

In the name of Allāh, the Beneficent,
the Merciful.

1. Say: O disbelievers!
2. I worship not that which you worship;
3. Nor worship you that which I worship
4. And I shall not worship that which you worship
5. Nor will you worship that which I worship.
6. Unto you your religion, and unto me my religion

EXPLANATION:

109:1. The *Kuffār* wanted an agreement with Rasūlullāh (S). Allāh (SWT) commanded Rasūlullāh (S) to tell them in clear terms that no such agreement was possible.

109:2. As Muslims, we cannot worship what the *Kuffār* worship. They worship idols and images and we worship one Allāh (SWT).

109:3. The *Kuffār* are not prepared to worship Allāh (SWT) alone; they love their idols.

109:4. Rasūlullāh (S), his *Ṣaḥābah* and the Muslims are forbidden to worship idols. They must never give up faith in Allāh (SWT) alone.

109:5. The *Kuffār* were never going to give up their idols because they did not understand that their idols were powerless.

109:6. The Muslims were not going to give up their firm belief in Allāh (SWT), nor were the *Kuffār* prepared to give up their idolatory. Rasūlullāh (S) and his *Ṣaḥābah* did not want to force the *Kuffār* to accept Islam, nor were they allowed to compromise their beliefs to please the *Kuffār*. Thus, Rasūlullāh (S) was commanded to leave them to their idol-worship, and in turn, the *Kuffār* were to allow the Muslims to practice their religion in peace.

WE HAVE LEARNED:

* Islam is the final and complete religion of Allāh (SWT).
* There can never be any compromise in matters of faith.
* But everyone must be left free to practice his own religion.

VOCABULARY

١٠٩-سُورَةُ ٱلْكَـٰفِرُونَ

١-قُلْ	*Qul*	say
يَـٰأَيُّهَا	*yā 'ayyuhā*	O you, O ye
اَلْكَـٰفِرُونَ	*'al-kāfirūn(a)*	the *kuffār*, disbelievers, who reject faith
٢-لَا أَعْبُدُ	*Lā 'a'budu*	I worship not, I don't worship
مَا تَعْبُدُونَ	*ma ta'budūn(a)*	what you worship
٣-وَلَا	*Wa-lā*	and nor, not
أَنْتُمْ	*'antum*	you (plural)
عَـٰبِدُونَ	*'ābidūna*	going to worship, will worship
مَا اَعْبُدُ	*mā 'a'bud(u)*	what I worship
٤-وَلَا	*Wa-lā*	and not
أَنَا	*'anā*	I (am, will)
عَابِدٌ	*'ābidun*	be a worshipper
مَّا عَبَدتُّمْ	*ma 'abadtum*	which you worship
٥-وَلَا	*Wa-lā*	And nor
أَنْتُمْ	*'antum*	you
عَـٰبِدُونَ	*'ābidūna*	will worship, are worshippers
مَا أَعْبُدُ	*mā 'a'bud(u)*	that I worship
٦-لَكُمْ	*La-kum*	for you, unto you
دِينُكُمْ	*dīnu-kum*	(is) your religion, is your *dīn*, is your way
وَلِىَ	*wa li-ya*	and for me, and to me
دِينِ	*dīn(i)*	my religion, my *dīn*, my way of life

سورة الكوثر

Lesson 8

AL-KAWTHAR, 108:1-3

THE ABUNDANCE / THE ABUNDANCE

Revealed in Makkah

TRANSLITERATION:	**ARABIC TEXT:**
Bismillāhi-(a)r-Raḥmāni-(a)r-Raḥīm	بِسْمِ اللَّهِ الرَّحْمَٰنِ الرَّحِيمِ
1. *'Innā 'a'ṭainā-ka-(a)l-Kawthar(a)*	-إِنَّا أَعْطَيْنَاكَ الْكَوْثَرَ ۝
2. *Faṣalli li Rabbi-ka wa-(a)nḥar*	.فَصَلِّ لِرَبِّكَ وَانْحَرْ ۝
3. *'Inna shāni'a-ka huwa-(a)l-'abtar(u)*	-إِنَّ شَانِئَكَ هُوَ الْأَبْتَرُ ۝

TRANSLATIONS:

In the name of Allāh, Most Gracious, Most Merciful.

1. To you have We granted the Fount (of Abundance).
2. Therefore to your Lord turn in Prayer and Sacrifice.
3. For he who hates you, he will be cut off (from Future Hope)

In the name of Allāh, the Beneficent, the Merciful.

1. Lo! We have given you Abundance;
2. So pray unto your Lord and sacrifice.
3. Lo! it is your insulter (and not you) who is without posterity.

EXPLANATION:

108:1. Rasūlullāh (S) had lost his son, Al-Qāsim, and as consolation, Allāh (SWT) gave him the river of *Kawthar* in *Jannah.* Allāh (SWT) will give the drink of *Al-Kawthar* to the people of *Jannah.* They will never feel thirsty afterward.

The literal Arabic translation of *Al-Kawthar* is "the Abundance." Thus, *Al-Kawthar* also means that Allāh (SWT) has blessed Rasūlullāh (S) in this world as well as in the *'Ākhirah.*

Rasūlullāh (S) had lost his son in this life, but he will be reunited with him in *Jannah.* He has also been blessed with an *'Ummah* that loves him more than children love their own parents. We remember him in our prayers. We say *Salla-Allāhu 'alai-hi wa-Sallam* when his name is mentioned.

108:2. Allāh (SWT) commands Rasūlullāh (S) to thank Him for His kindness by offering *salāh* and sacrifice. Following Rasūlūllah's example, we must thank Him by offering prayer. We must thank Allāh (SWT) by doing the things that He has commanded us to do, and by not doing those things that Allāh (SWT) has forbidden.

We should pay thanks to Allāh (SWT) by sacrificing the things that we love most for those who need them more than we do.

108:3. It is 'Abū Jahl, the *Kuffār* and the enemies of Islam who have been cut off. No one follows them, prays for them or otherwise remembers them.

WE HAVE LEARNED:

* Allāh (SWT) has blessed Rasūlullāh (S) with His choicest blessings.
* The followers of Rasūlullāh (S) will receive the drink of *Al-Kawthar* in *Jannah.*
* The 'Ummah loves Rasūlullāh (S) and remembers him by following his *Sunnah.*

VOCABULARY

١٠٨-سُورَةُ ٱلكَوثَر

١-إِنَّا	*'Innā*	Indeed We
أَعْطَيْنَاكَ	*'a'ṭainā-ka*	(We) have given you
الكَوثَرَ	*'al-kawthar (a)*	the abundance, the river *kawthar* in Paradise
٢-فَصَلِّ	*Fa-ṣalli*	So, pray
لِرَبِّكَ	*li-Rabbi-ka*	for your Lord
وَٱنْحَرْ	*wa-nḥar*	and sacrifice
٣-إِنَّ	*'Inna*	Lo! indeed, surely
شَانِئَكَ	*shāni' a-ka*	your insulter, hater, enemy
هُوَ	*huwa*	who, he (is)
الأَبْتَرُ	*'al-'abtar(u)*	the one cut off without posterity (children)

سُورَةُ الْمَاعُونِ

Lesson 9

AL-MĀ`ŪN, 107:1-7

THE NEIGHBORLY ASSISTANCE / SMALL KINDNESSES

Revealed in Makkah

INTRODUCTION:

The people of Makkah denied the *'Ākhirah*. They claimed that there was no life after death, and that they were not responsible to Allāh (SWT) for their actions. Those who do not believe in the *'Ākhirah* feel that they can do what they want. They do not feed the poor or help the needy.

A believer, on the other hand, is one who believes in the *'Ākhirah* and helps others, just to gain the pleasure of Allāh (SWT).

TRANSLITERATION:	**ARABIC TEXT:**
Bismillāhi-(a)r-Raḥmāni-(a)r-Raḥīm	بِسْمِ اللهِ الرَّحْمٰنِ الرَّحِيمِ
1. *'Ara'ait-alladhī yukadh-dhibu bi-(a)d-dīn(i)*	أَرَأَيْتَ الَّذِي يُكَذِّبُ بِالدِّينِ ۝-
2. *Fa dhālika-lladhī yadu``ul-yatīm(a)*	فَذٰلِكَ الَّذِي يَدُعُّ الْيَتِيمَ ۝-
3. *Wa-lā yaḥuḍḍu `alā ṭa`āmi-(a)l-miskīn(i)*	وَلَا يَحُضُّ عَلٰى طَعَامِ الْمِسْكِينِ ۝-
4. *Fa wailu-(an)-li-l muṣallīn (a)*	فَوَيْلٌ لِّلْمُصَلِّينَ ۝-
5. *'Alladhīna hum `an ṣalāti-him sāhūn(a)*	الَّذِينَ هُمْ عَن صَلَاتِهِمْ سَاهُونَ ۝-
6. *'Alladhīna hum yurā'ūn(a)*	الَّذِينَ هُمْ يُرَآءُونَ ۝-
7. *Wa yamna`ūna-(a)l-mā`ūn(a)*	وَيَمْنَعُونَ الْمَاعُونَ ۝-

TRANSLATIONS:

In the name of Allāh, Most Gracious, Most Merciful.

1. Do you see the one who denies the Judgment (to come)?

In the name of Allāh, the Beneficent, the Merciful.

1. Have you observed him who belies religion?

2. Then such is the man who repulses the orphan (with harshness)	2. That is he who repels the orphan,
3. And encourages not the feeding of the indigent.	3. And urges not the feeding of the needy.
4. So woe to the worshippers.	4. Ah, woe unto worshippers.
5. Who are neglectful of their Prayers.	5. Who are heedless of their prayers;
6. Those who (want but) to be seen (of men).	6. Who would be seen (at worship).
7. But refuse (to supply) (even) neighborly needs.	7. Yet refuse small kindnesses!

EXPLANATION:

107:1. *Ad-Dīn* means faith in the *'Ākhirah*, the Day of Judgment. *Ad-Dīn* is also the religion of Islam. This *Sūrah* speaks about two kinds of people: those who deny the *'Ākhirah* and those who deny the religion of Islam.

107:2. A person who denies Allāh (SWT) does not try to please Him. Because he does not believe in the *'Ākhirah*, he does not think that he will ever be judged. This is why such a person may do such selfish acts as reject the orphans or the needy.

107:3. Such people do not feed the hungry. They feel that they will lose their money by doing so. Rasūlullāh (S) has told us: "Money spent in the way of Allāh (SWT) does not decrease our wealth but, rather, it increases it."

107:4. Offering the *ṣalāh* is a *farḍ* upon every adult Muslim.

107:5. There are many who call themselves Muslims, yet do not offer the *ṣalāh*, or if they do so,they become easily distracted. This is not true prayer, and Allāh (SWT) warns us that such people will suffer.

107:6. Allāh (SWT) also warns people who pray for show, rather than to please Allāh (SWT). These people are hypocrites, or *munāfiqūn*.

107:7. They say that they believe in Allāh (SWT) and in the *'Akhirah*, but in reality, they do not, because they refuse to show even a little kindness when asked to. Islam teaches us to be helpful to others, even if it causes us discomfort. We have a duty to our neighbors. We should be ready to help them with anything that they may need.

VOCABULARY

١٠٧-سُورَةُ ٱلْمَاعُون

١-أرَءَيْتَ	*'Ara'aita*	Did you see?
اَلَّذِى	*'alladhi*	the one who, him who
يُكَذِّبُ	*yukadhdhibu*	(He) denies, refutes
بِٱلدِّين	*bi-(a)d-Dīn(i)*	(to) the religion, the day of Judgment
٢-فَذٰلِكَ	*Fa-dhālika*	So , that one is
اَلَّذِى	*'alladhī*	the one who
يَدُعُّ	*yadu''u*	(He) repels, pushes, turns away
اَلْيَتِيمَ	*'al-yatīm(a)*	the orphan
٣-وَلَا يَحُضُّ	*Walā yahuddu*	And does not urge
عَلَىٰ طَعَامِ	*'ala ṭa'āmi*	to the feeding (of)
اَلْمِسْكِين	*'al-miskīn(i)*	the needy, poor
٤-فَوَيْلٌ	*Fawailun*	So, woe
لِلْمُصَلِّينَ	*li-(a)l-muṣallīn(a)*	to the worshippers
٥-اَلَّذِينَ هُمْ	*'Alladhīna hum*	Those people who
عَنْ	*'an*	from
صَلَاتِهِمْ	*ṣalāti-him*	their *ṣalah*, their prayer
سَاهُونَ	*sāhūn(a)*	heedless, forgetful

٦-اَلَّذِينَ	*'Alla<u>dh</u>ina*	who, those people
هُمْ يُرَآءُونَ	*hum yurā'ūna*	they show off, those would be seen
٧-وَيَمْنَعُونَ	*Wa-yamna'ūna*	and they refuse, deny
اَلْمَاعُونَ	*'al-mā'ūn(a)*	the utensils, neighborly needs, small kindnesses

Lesson 10

سُورَةُ قُرَيْشٍ

QURAISH, 106:1-4

THE TRIBE OF QURAISH / WINTER OR QURAISH

Revealed in Makkah

INTRODUCTION:

The Quraish were caretakers of Ka'bah and looked after the pilgrims who came to Makkah. The Arabs respected the Quraish and accepted them as their leaders. Because of treaties with other Arab tribes, the caravans of the Quraish were safeguarded from attack by them.

The Quraish were traders and they travelled with their trade caravans to other cities. During the winter, they went to Yemen where the weather was warmer than in Makkah, and during the summer, they travelled to Syria which was cooler at this time. Travel and trade made the Quraish wealthy. Security allowed them to enjoy peaceful lives. Allāh (SWT) wanted the Quraish to thank Him for the many blessings that He had given them. He commanded the Quraish to give up their *shirk* and to believe in *Tawḥīd* and to worship Him alone.

TRANSLITERATION:	**ARABIC TEXT:**
Bismillāhi-(a)r-Raḥmāni-(a)r-Raḥīm(i)	بِسْمِ اللَّهِ الرَّحْمَٰنِ الرَّحِيمِ
1. *Li 'īlāfi Quraishin*	لِإِيلَافِ قُرَيْشٍ ۝
2. *'Īlāfi-him riḥlata-sh-shitā'i wa-(a)ṣ-ṣaif(i)*	إِيلَافِهِمْ رِحْلَةَ الشِّتَاءِ وَالصَّيْفِ ۝
3. *Fal-ya'budū Rabba hādha-(a)l-bait(i)*	فَلْيَعْبُدُوا رَبَّ هَٰذَا الْبَيْتِ ۝
4. *'Alladhī 'aṭ'ama-hum min jū'in*	الَّذِي أَطْعَمَهُمْ مِنْ جُوعٍ
wa 'āmana-hum-min khawf(in)	وَآمَنَهُمْ مِنْ خَوْفٍ ۝

TRANSLATIONS:

In the name of Allāh, Most Gracious, Most Merciful.

1. For the covenants (of security and safeguard enjoyed) by the Quraish,

In the name of Allāh, the Beneficent, the Merciful.

1. For the taming of Quraish

2. Their covenants (covering) journeys by winter and summer,	2. For their taming (We cause) the caravans to set forth in winter and summer.
3. Let them adore the Lord of this House,	3. So let them worship the Lord of this House,
4. Who provides them with food against hunger and with security against fear (of danger).	4. Who has fed them against hunger, and has made them safe from fear.

EXPLANATION:

106:1. "Covenants of Quraish" refers to the agreements the Quraish had with other Arab tribes for peace and security. These treaties allowed the Quraish to continue their trading with other tribes, without fear of robbery or any endangerment to their lives.

106:2. These agreements permitted the Quraish to travel south in winter and north during the summer, at their own convenience. The Quraish lived peaceful lives at home, and were free and secure during their travels. Allāh (SWT) had given these special advantages to the Quraish. Therefore, the Quraish were asked to worship Allāh (SWT) alone.

106:3. The Ka'bah is known as *Bait Allāh*, the 'House of Allāh (SWT).' The Quraish had made *Bait Allāh* a house of idols. The Quraish were commanded to give up *shirk* and to worship Allāh (SWT) alone.

116:4. Idols have no power. No one has power except Allāh (SWT). It is He who feeds us when we are hungry. The Quraish were wealthy, and they had good food to eat because Allāh (SWT) provided for them. It was also Allāh (SWT) who had given them peace and security, and prestige among the Arabs as caretakers of the Ka'bah. All the Arabs respected the Quraish and accepted their leadership, which made the Quraish bold and fearless.

WE HAVE LEARNED:

* Allāh (SWT) has blessed us with His special favors, we must thank Him and worship Him alone.
* We must recognize Allāh (SWT) as our *Rabb*, our Creator, Sustainer and Protector.
* He is the Only One who feeds us in hunger and gives us peace from fear.

VOCABULARY

١٠٦-سُورَةُ قُرَيْشٍ

١-لِإِيلَٰفِ	*Li 'ilāfi*	For the covenants, the agreements
قُرَيْشٍ	*Quraish(in)*	the family of Quraish
٢-إِلَٰفِهِمْ	*'Īlāfi-him*	Their covenants, their agreements
رِحْلَةَ	*riḥlata*	journey (of)
ٱلشِّتَآءِ	*'ash-shitā'(i)*	The winter
وَٱلصَّيْفِ	*wa-(a)ṣ-ṣaif(i)*	and the summer
٣-فَلْيَعْبُدُوا	*Fal-ya'budū*	So, they should worship, So let them adore
رَبَّ	*Rabb(a)*	The Lord (of)
هَٰذَا	*hādha*	this,
ٱلْبَيْتِ	*Al-Bait(i)*	the House
٤-ٱلَّذِى	*'Alladhī*	Who, He Who
أَطْعَمَهُمْ	*'aṭ'ama-hum*	gave them food, fed them
مِّن جُوعٍ	*min jū'(in)*	(against) hunger
وَءَامَنَهُمْ	*wa-' āmana-hum*	and made them secure, gave them safety
مِّنْ خَوْفٍ	*min khawf (in)*	from fear, against fear

Lesson 11

سُورَةُ الفِيلِ

AL-FĪL, 105:1-5

THE ELEPHANT / THE ELEPHANT

Revealed in Makkah

INTRODUCTION:

This *Sūrah* relates the story of Abraha, the ruler of Yemen, who invaded Makkah with the intention of destroying the Ka`bah. Abraha's army was led by elephants. Because of this fact, the Qur'ān calls the invaders the "People of the Elephant."

This *Sūrah* tells us how Allah (SWT) destroyed Abraha's army with tiny birds and thus saved the Ka`bah. At the time of this Revelation, many Makkans who remembered this incident were still alive, and they retold this story over and over to their children.

TRANSLITERATION:

Bismillāhi-(a)r-Raḥmāni-(a)r-Raḥīm — بِسْمِ ٱللَّهِ ٱلرَّحْمَٰنِ ٱلرَّحِيمِ

1. *'Alam tara kaifa fa`ala Rabbu-ka bi-'Aṣḥābi-(a)l-fīl(i)* — أَلَمْ تَرَ كَيْفَ فَعَلَ رَبُّكَ بِأَصْحَٰبِ ٱلْفِيلِ ۝

2. *'Alam yaj`al kaida-hum fī taḍlīl(in)* — أَلَمْ يَجْعَلْ كَيْدَهُمْ فِى تَضْلِيلٍ ۝

3. *Wa 'arsala `alai-him ṭairan 'abābīl(a)* — وَأَرْسَلَ عَلَيْهِمْ طَيْرًا أَبَابِيلَ ۝

4. *Tarmī-him bi-ḥijāratin min sijjīl(in)* — تَرْمِيهِم بِحِجَارَةٍ مِّن سِجِّيلٍ ۝

5. *Fa-ja`ala-hum ka`aṣfin ma'kul(in)* — فَجَعَلَهُمْ كَعَصْفٍ مَّأْكُولٍ ۝

TRANSLATIONS:

In the name of Allāh, Most Gracious,
Most Merciful.
1. Do you not see how your Lord
   dealt with the Companions of the Elephant?

In the name of Allāh, the Beneficent,
the Merciful.
1. Have you not seen how your Lord
   dealt with the owners of the Elephant?

2. Did He not make their treacherous plan go astray?
3. And He sent against them Flights of Birds,
4. Striking them with stones of baked clay.
5. Then did He make them like an empty field of stalks and straw, (of which the corn) has been eaten up.

2. Did he not bring their stratagem to naught,
3. And send against them swarms of flying creatures,
4. Which pelted them with stones of baked clay,
5. And made them like green crops devoured (by cattle)?

EXPLANATION:

105:1. This strange incident had occured not long ago. Many people who witnessed it were living when this *Sūrah* was revealed. The younger people of Makkah had heard the story from their parents and grandparents. The tale was known around the entire Arabian peninsula. In this *Sūrah*, Allāh (SWT) reminds Rasūlullāh (S) and his people of that incident; when He had dealt with "the people of the elephant."

105:2. The plan of Abraha was to invade Makkah and destroy the Ka'bah. Instead, Allāh (SWT) destroyed his plan.

105:3. Allāh (SWT) sent small birds to destroy an army of strong elephants.

105:4. The birds carried small stones in their beaks to pelt Abraha's army with.

105:5. The elephants could not move, and the army of Abraha dispersed in confusion. They were pelted with stones that cut them. The disbelievers resembled straw, after it has been chewed by animals. Those who managed to return home died of various diseases. It was a total destruction of Abraha's army.

WE HAVE LEARNED:

* No power, no matter what, can harm anyone if Allāh protects that one.
* Allāh is the Protector and Lord, and the believers must fear no one but Him.
* He can invite the help of the smallest of His creatures to defeat the biggest of His enemies.

VOCABULARY

١٠٥-سُورَةُ ٱلفِيْلِ

١-أَلَمْ تَرَ	*'Alam tara*	Have you not seen ?
كَيْفَ	*kaifa*	how, what
فَعَلَ	*fa'ala*	(he) dealt, (he) did
رَبُّكَ	*Rabbu-ka*	your Lord
بِ	*bi*	with
أَصْحَٰبِ ٱلفِيلِ	*'Aṣḥābi-(a)lfīl(i)*	(the) Companions of the Elephant, Owners of the Elephant
٢-أَلَمْ يَجْعَلْ	*'Alam yaj'al*	Did He not make
كَيْدَهُمْ	*kaida-hum*	their strategy, evil plan, their plotting
فِي تَضْلِيلٍ	*fi taḍlīl(in)*	in failure, go astray
٣-وَأَرْسَلَ	*Wa- 'arsala*	And (He) sent
عَلَيْهِمْ	*'alai-him*	against them (Lit. "on them")
طَيْرًا	*ṭairan*	birds
أَبَابِيْلَ	*'abābīl(a)*	flights, groups
٤-تَرْمِيهِمْ	*Tarmī-him*	Pelting, striking them
بِحِجَارَةٍ	*bi-ḥijāratin*	with stones
مِّن سِجِّيلٍ	*min sijjīl(in)*	of baked clay (Lit. "from baked clay")
٥-فَجَعَلَهُمْ	*Fa-ja'ala-hum*	Then He made them
كَعَصْفٍ	*ka-'aṣf(in)*	like green crop, stray
مَّأكُولٍ	*ma'kūl(in)*	chewed up, eaten up

Lesson 12

سُورَةُ الهُمَزَة
آياتها ٩ — ترتيبها ١٠٤

AL-HUMAZAH, 104:1-9:

THE SCANDAL-MONGER / THE TRADUCER

Revealed in Makkah

INTRODUCTION:

This early Makkan *Sūrah* condemns some of the evils prevalent in Makkan society, such as the spreading of scandals, backbiting and the hoarding of wealth. Those who reject the Truth and are involved in these social evils will receive Divine punishment on the Day of Judgment.

TRANSLITERATION:	**ARABIC TEXT**:
Bismillāhi-(a)r-Raḥmāni-(a)r-Raḥīm(i)	بِسْمِ اللَّهِ الرَّحْمَٰنِ الرَّحِيمِ
1. *Wailul-li-kulli humazati-l-lumazah(ti)*	وَيْلٌ لِّكُلِّ هُمَزَةٍ لُّمَزَةٍ ۝ -1
2. *'Alladhī jama'a mālan wa 'addadah(u)*	الَّذِي جَمَعَ مَالًا وَعَدَّدَهُ ۝ -2
3. *Yaḥsabu 'anna māla-hū 'akhladah(u)*	يَحْسَبُ أَنَّ مَالَهُ أَخْلَدَهُ ۝ -3
4. *Kallā la-yumbadhanna fi-(a)l-ḥuṭamah(ti)*	كَلَّا لَيُنبَذَنَّ فِي الْحُطَمَةِ ۝ -4
5. *Wa-mā 'adrā-ka ma-(a)l-ḥuṭamah(tu)*	وَمَا أَدْرَاكَ مَا الْحُطَمَةُ ۝ -5
6. *Nāru-(A)llāhi-(a)l-mūqadah(tu)*	نَارُ اللَّهِ الْمُوقَدَةُ ۝ -6
7. *Allatī taṭṭali'u 'ala-(a)l-'af'idah(ti)*	الَّتِي تَطَّلِعُ عَلَى الْأَفْئِدَةِ ۝ -7
8. *'Inna-hā 'alai-him mu'ṣadah(tun)*	إِنَّهَا عَلَيْهِم مُّؤْصَدَةٌ ۝ -8
9. *Fī 'amadin mumaddadah(tin)*	فِي عَمَدٍ مُّمَدَّدَةٍ ۝ -9

TRANSLATIONS:

In the name of Allāh, Most Gracious,
Most Merciful.

1. Woe to every (kind of) scandalmonger and backbiter,
2. Who piles up wealth And lays it by,
3. Thinking that his wealth would make him last forever!
4. By no means! He will be sure to be thrown into that which breaks to pieces.
5. And what will explain to you that which breaks to pieces?
6. (It is) the Fire of (the Wrath of) Allāh kindled (to a blaze),
7. That which does mount (right) to the hearts.
8. It shall be made into a vault over them,
9. In columns outstretched.

In the name of Allāh, the Beneficent,
the Merciful.

1. Woe unto every slandering traducer,
2. Who has gathered wealth (of this world) and arranged it.
3. He thinks that his wealth will render him immortal.
4. Nay, but verily he will be flung to the Consuming One,
5. Ah, what will convey unto you what the Consuming One is!
6. (It is) the fire of Allāh, kindled,
7. Which leaps up over the hearts (of men)
8. Lo! it is closed in on them
9. In outstretched columns.

EXPLANATION:

104:1.The Arabic terms *Humazah* and *Lumazah* refer to one who loves to spread scandals about others. Such a person looks down upon other people, creates rumors, makes false accusations, backbites, and causes hatred among people.

104:2. *Humazah* and *Lumazah* accumulate and hoard wealth. They do not spend their money for the benefit of their relatives, the needy or the poor. They do not contribute their wealth to charities that benefit the welfare of others. They receive special pleasure in seeing their wealth grow.

104:3. Such people believe that their wealth will last forever. Pride in their possessions make them forget that this life will one day come to an end, and that they will have to leave all their wealth and other worldly things behind. Their wealth makes them feel superior to others and they become proud and arrogant.

104:4-6. Because of their greed, love of scandal and their arrogance, they will be thrown into *Ḥutamah*, the blazing Fire of Hell. The Arabic term ***Ḥutamah*** is loosely translated as being a thing which breaks everything else into pieces. The Fire of Hell, especially kindled by Allāh (SWT) for such arrogant and scandalous people, will break their minds and bodies into pieces.

104-7-8. The Fire will jump to the heart, because the ***humazah*** and ***lumazah*** possess evil hearts. This fire jumps to the heart in this world also: it is the fire of jealousy and arrogance that burns such people.

104:9. The blazing flames of the fire of *Ḥutamah* are high, like a huge column.

WE HAVE LEARNED:

* Our wealth, whether we inherit it or have earned it, is a gift from Allāh (SWT).
* We must not be excessively proud of our wealth and behave arrogantly toward others.
* For those who love scandal and are arrogant, Allāh's anger, the *Ḥutamah,* awaits them on the Day of Judgment.

VOCABULARY

١٠٤: سُورَةُ ٱلهُمَزَةِ

١-وَيلٌ	*Wailun*	Woe
لِ	*li*	for, to
كُلِّ	*kulli*	every (all)
هُمَزَةٍ	*humazatin*	scandal monger, slandering person
لُمَزَةٍ	*lumazah(tin)*	traducer, backbiter
٢-ٱلَّذِى	*'Alladhī*	Who, he who
جَمَعَ	*jama'a*	piled up, gathered
مَالاً	*mālan*	wealth, money
وَعَدَّدَهُ	*wa-'addada-h(u)*	and counted it, and arranged it
٣-يَحْسَبُ	*Yaḥsabu*	He thinks
أَنَّ	*'anna*	that indeed
مَالَهُ	*māla-hū*	his wealth
أَخْلَدَهُ	*'akhlada-h(u)*	make him immortal, make him live forever

٤-كَلاَّ	*Kallā*	Nay, surely not
لَيُنْبَذَنَّ	*la-yamba<u>dh</u>anna*	surely he will be thrown, he will be flung
فِى	*fī*	into
اَلْحُطَمَةِ	*'al-ḥuṭamah(ti)*	consuming one, what breaks every thing into pieces
٥-وَمَا	*Wa-mā*	And what
اَدْرٰكَ	*'adrā-ka*	will explain to you, convey to you
مَا ٱلْحُطَمَةُ	*ma-(a)l-ḥuṭamah(tu)*	what is the consuming one, that which breaks every thing into pieces
٦-نَارُ	*Nār(u)*	The fire (of)
اَللّٰهِ	*'Allāh(i)*	(of) Allah
اَلْمُوقَدَةُ	*'al-mūqadah (tu)*	kindled
٧-اَلَّتِى	*'Allatī*	Which
تَطَّلِعُ	*taṭṭali'u*	leaps up, jumps up
عَلَى	*'Alā*	on
اَلأَفْئِدَةِ	*'al-'af'idah(ti)*	the hearts
٨-إِنَّهَا	*'Inna-hā*	Indeed it (is)
عَلَيْهِمْ	*'alai-him*	on them
مُؤْصَدَةٌ	*mu'ṣadat(un)*	made into vault, closed in
٩-فِى عَمَدٍ	*Fī 'amad(in)*	In columns
مُمَدَّدَةٍ	*mumaddadah(tin)*	outstretched

Lesson 13 سُورَةُ الْعَصْرِ

AL-'AṢR, 103:1-3

THE TIME / THE DECLINING DAY

Revealed in Makkah

INTRODUCTION:

This is an early Makkan *Sūrah*. It utilizes Time as a witness to human history. Time has seen the destruction of evil and the dominance of good.

TRANSLITERATION:	ARABIC TEXT:
Bismillāhi-(a)r-Raḥmāni-(a)r-Raḥīm(i)	بِسْمِ اللهِ الرَّحْمٰنِ الرَّحِيْمِ
1. *Wa-(a)l-'Aṣr(i)*	١- وَالْعَصْرِ ۝
2. *'Inna-(a)l-'insāna la-fī khusr(in)*	٢- إِنَّ الْإِنْسَانَ لَفِيْ خُسْرٍ ۝
3. *'Illa-(a)l-ladhīna 'āmanū wa 'amilu-(a)ṣ-ṣāliḥāti*	٣- إِلَّا الَّذِيْنَ اٰمَنُوْا وَعَمِلُوا الصّٰلِحٰتِ
wa tawāṣaw bi-l-ḥaqqi wa tawāṣaw bi-(a)ṣ-ṣabr(i)	وَتَوَاصَوْا بِالْحَقِّ ۙ وَتَوَاصَوْا بِالصَّبْرِ ۝

TRANSLATIONS:

In the name of Allāh, Most Gracious, Most Merciful.

1. By (the Token of) Time (through the Ages),
2. Truly Man is in Loss,
3. Except such as have Faith,
   and do righteous deeds, and (join together)
   in the mutual teaching of Truth,
   and of Patience and Constancy.

In the name of Allāh, the Beneficent, the Merciful.

1. By the declining day,
2. Lo! man is in a state of loss,
3. Save those who believe
   and do good works, and exhort
   one another to truth;
   exhort one another to endurance.

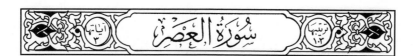

EXPLANATION:

103:1.The Arabic term *Al-'Aṣr* means "time," as it has passed, from the moment of the first creation. It is also the name given to the time of the afternoon prayer. Time continues its passage now, as it shall continue to pass until the Day of Judgment. Time is a creation of Allāh (SWT). All His creations are affected by time in one way or another. Only He is not controlled by time.

103:2. Time is witness to what has passed in human history. It has seen life and death, success and failure, rise and fall and the comings and goings of individuals and of communities. It has seen everything ultimately come to an end.

103:3. Time has witnessed that all human beings are at loss except for those who have the following four characteristics.

Those who believe,
Those who do good deeds,
Those who enjoin others to do good deeds,
Those who encourage others to remain patient during adversity.

"Belief" is an individual characterstic. The remaining three characteristics are found in both, the individual and in the society.

Islam teaches us that it is not enough to lead one's life righteously. As Muslims, we have a responsibility to work toward the establishment of a just and righteous society. Individuals and communities that possess such qualities will be successful in this world and in the Hereafter.

WE HAVE LEARNED:

* No matter how long we live, death is the ultimate fate for all of us.
* Therefore, we must act righteously and follow Allāh's commandments.
* This is the only way we may be successful in this world and in the Hereafter.

UNDERSTANDING OF A SCHOLAR

Imām Rāzī, a famous *Mufassir*, has quoted a scholar as saying, "I understood the meaning of this *Sūrah* through listening to an ice vendor. On a hot day, as his ice melted quickly, he called people's attention by saying: O people, have mercy on a person whose only wealth is melting away fast."

VOCABULARY

١٠٣- سُورَةُ ٱلعَصْرِ

١-وَٱلعَصْرِ	*Wa-(a)l-'aṣri*	By the Time, by the Declining Time
٢-إِنَّ	*'Inna*	indeed, surely, verily
اَلإِنسَانَ	*'al-'insān(a)*	human-kind, men
لَفِى	*la-fī*	surely are in
خُسْرٍ	*khusr(in)*	loss, state of loss
٣-إِلاَّ	*'Illa*	save, except
اَلَّذِيْنَ	*'alladhīna*	such as, those
امَنُوا	*'āmanū*	(Those) who believe
وَعَمِلُوا	*wa-'amilū*	and do, and act
اَلصَّلِحٰتِ	*'aṣ-ṣāliḥāti*	the good works, righteous deeds
وَتَوَاصَوْا	*wa-tawāṣaw*	and exhort one another, encourge one another
بِٱلْحَقِّ	*bi-(a)l-ḥaqqi*	in the Truth, in the teaching of Truth
وَتَوَاصَوْا	*wa-tawāṣaw*	and exhort one another, encourage one another
بِٱلصَّبْرِ	*Bi-(a)ṣ-ṣabr(i)*	endurance, patience

Lesson 14

سُورَةُ التَّكَاثُرِ

AT-TAKĀTHUR, 102:1-8

PILING UP / RIVALRY IN WORDLY INCREASE

Revealed in Makkah

INTRODUCTION:

This is an early Makkan *Sūrah*. It describes the dangers of greed and hoarding of worldly goods. Our involvement with worldly concerns often results in the neglect of our responsibilities to Allāh (SWT) and to our fellow human beings. Allāh's blessings are too numerous to mention, we can never offer enough thanks for them. On the Day of Judgment, we shall account for every favor that Allāh (SWT) has blessed us with.

TRANSLITERATION:	**ARABIC TEXT**:
Bismillāhi-(a)r-Raḥmāni-(a)r-Raḥīm	بِسْمِ اللهِ الرَّحْمٰنِ الرَّحِيْمِ
1. *'Alhākumu-(a)t-takāthur(u)*	أَلْهٰكُمُ التَّكَاثُرُ ۝
2. *Ḥattā zurtumu-(a)l-maqābir(a)*	حَتّٰى زُرْتُمُ الْمَقَابِرَ ۝
3. *Kallā sawfa ta`lamūn(a)*	كَلَّا سَوْفَ تَعْلَمُوْنَ ۝
4. *Thumma kallā sawfa ta`lamūn(a)*	ثُمَّ كَلَّا سَوْفَ تَعْلَمُوْنَ ۝
5. *Kallā law ta`lamūna `ilma-(a)l-yaqīn(i)*	كَلَّا لَوْ تَعْلَمُوْنَ عِلْمَ الْيَقِيْنِ ۝
6. *La-tarawunna-(a)l-jaḥīm(a)*	لَتَرَوُنَّ الْجَحِيْمَ ۝
7. *Thumma la-tarawunna-hā `aina-(a)l-yaqīn(i)*	ثُمَّ لَتَرَوُنَّهَا عَيْنَ الْيَقِيْنِ ۝
8. *Thumma la-tus'alunna yawma'idhin `ani-(a)n-na`īm(i).*	ثُمَّ لَتُسْئَلُنَّ يَوْمَئِذٍ عَنِ النَّعِيْمِ ۝

TRANSLATIONS:

In the name of Allāh, Most Gracious,
Most Merciful.

1. The mutual rivalry for piling up (the good things of this world) diverts you (from the more serious things),
2. Until you visit the graves.
3. But no, you soon shall know (the reality)
4. Again, you soon shall know!
5. No, were you to know with certainty of mind, (you would beware!).
6. You shall certainly see Hell-fire!
7. Again, you shall see it with certainty of sight
8. Then shall you be questioned that Day about the joy (you indulged in!)

In the name of Allāh, the Beneficent,
the Merciful.

1. Rivalry in worldly increase distracts you
2. Until you come to the graves.
3. Nay, but you will come to know!
4. Nay, but you will come to know!
5. Nay, would that you knew (now) with sure knowledge!
6. For you will behold hell-fire.
7. Again, you will behold it with sure vision.
8. Then, on that day, you will be asked concerning pleasure.

EXPLANATION:

102:1. The term *takāthur* is the desire to gain more and more of those things, that we feel will give us comfort and security, such as: wealth, power, position and influence. Our efforts of *takāthur*, the increase in pleasurable things of this world, distract us from remembering our duties to Allāh (SWT) and to our fellow human beings. Only *Qanā'ah* (contentment) and sharing our blessings with others could help us lead a peaceful life.

102:2-7. Those people involved in *takāthur* continue to hoard pleasurable things until they die. After death, they will see, with the certainty of their own eyes, the Fire of Hell. They had been so busy increasing their possessions, that they had no time to prepare for the life after death.

102-8. On the Day of Judgment all of us will be questioned about our actions. Those who spent their life in *takāthur,* (increasing, piling up, enjoying and carelessly wasting resources) will be answerable to Allāh (SWT) for all that they did in this world.

WE HAVE LEARNED:

* Our greed for worldly goods causes in us a desire to accumulate more and more.
* Only *qanā'ah*, or contentment and sharing our blessings with others, can help us in this life.
* We shall be accountable to Allāh (SWT) for whatever gifts He blesses us with.

VOCABULARY

١٠٢- سُورَةُ ٱلتَّكَاثُر

١-اَلْهَٰكُمُ	'*Alhā-kumu*	Distracts you
اَلتَّكَاثُرُ	'*at-takāthur(u)*	rivalry in wordly increase
٢-حَتَّىٰ	*Ḥattā*	Until
زُرْتُمُ	*zurtum(u)*	you visit, you come to
اَلْمَقَابِرَ	'*al-maqābir(a)*	the graves
٣-كَلَّا	*Kallā*	But no, nay
سَوْفَ تَعْلَمُونَ	*sawfa ta'lamūn(a)*	(soon) you will know
٤-ثُمَّ كَلَّا	*Thumma kallā*	And then, again but no, nay
سَوْفَ تَعْلَمُونَ	*Sawfa ta'lamūn(a)*	(soon) you will know
٥-كَلَّا لَوْ	*Kallā law*	But no, if
تَعْلَمُونَ	*ta'lamūna*	you will know
عِلْمَ ٱلْيَقِينِ	'*ilma '(a)l-yaqīn(i)*	knowledge of certainty, sure
٦-لَتَرَوُنَّ	*La-tarawunna*	You shall certainly see
اَلْجَحِيمَ	*(a)l-jaḥīm(a)*	hell-fire
٧-ثُمَّ	*Thumma*	But again
لَتَرَوُنَّهَا	*la-tarawunna-hā*	you shall certainly see it
عَيْنَ ٱلْيَقِينِ	'*aina-(a)l-yaqīn(i)*	sight of certainty, sure
٨-ثُمَّ	*Thumma*	Then
لَتُسْئَلُنَّ	*la-tus'alunna*	you shall be surely asked
يَوْمَئِذٍ	*yawma'idhin*	on that day
عَنِ ٱلنَّعِيمِ	'*ani -(a)na'īm(i)*	about the joy, concerning the pleasure

Lesson 15

سُورَةُ الْقَارِعَةِ

AL-QĀRI'AH, 101:1-11

THE DAY OF NOISE AND CLAMOR / THE CALAMITY

Revealed in Makkah

INTRODUCTION:

This is an early Makkan *Sūrah*. It describes the events of the Day of Judgment. On this Day, the world will come to an end by means of a violent convulsion, and Allāh (SWT) will establish His final Justice.

TRANSLITERATION:	**ARABIC TEXT:**
Bismillāhi-(a)r-Raḥmāni-(a)r-Raḥīm(i)	بِسْمِ اللَّهِ الرَّحْمَٰنِ الرَّحِيمِ
1. *'Al-qāri'**ah**(tu)*	الْقَارِعَةُ ۝
2. *Ma-(a)l-qāri'**ah**(tu)*	مَا الْقَارِعَةُ ۝
3. *Wa mā 'adrā-ka ma-(a)l-qāri'**ah**(tu)*	وَمَا أَدْرَاكَ مَا الْقَارِعَةُ ۝
4. *Yawma yakūnu-(a)n- nāsu ka-(a)lfarāshi-(a)l-mabthūth(i)*	يَوْمَ يَكُونُ النَّاسُ كَالْفَرَاشِ الْمَبْثُوثِ ۝
5. *Wa takūnu-(a)l-jibālu ka-(a)l-'ihni-(a)l-manfūsh(i)*	وَتَكُونُ الْجِبَالُ كَالْعِهْنِ الْمَنْفُوشِ ۝
6. *Fa-'ammā man thaqulat mawāzīnu-hū*	فَأَمَّا مَنْ ثَقُلَتْ مَوَازِينُهُ ۝
7. *Fa-huwa fī 'īshatin rāḍiyah(tin)*	فَهُوَ فِي عِيشَةٍ رَاضِيَةٍ ۝
8. *Wa-'ammā man khaffat mawāzīnu-hū*	وَأَمَّا مَنْ خَفَّتْ مَوَازِينُهُ ۝
9. *Fa-'ummu-hū hāwiyah(tun)*	فَأُمُّهُ هَاوِيَةٌ ۝
10. *Wa mā 'adrā-ka mā-hiyah*	وَمَا أَدْرَاكَ مَا هِيَهْ ۝
11. *Nārun ḥāmiyah(tun)*	نَارٌ حَامِيَةٌ ۝

TRANSLATIONS:

In the name of Allāh, Most Gracious,
Most Merciful.

1. The (Day) of Noise and Clamour:
2. What is the (Day) of Noise and Clamour?
3. And what will explain to you what the (Day) of Noise and Clamour is?
4. (It is) a Day on which men will be like moths scattered about,
5. And the mountains will be like carded wool.
6. Then, he whose Balance (of good deeds) will be found heavy,
7. Will be in a Life of good pleasure and satisfaction.
8. But he whose Balance (of good deeds) will be (found) light-
9. Will have his home in a (bottomless) Pit.
10. And what will explain to you what this is?
11. (It is) a Fire blazing fiercely!

In the name of Allāh, the Beneficent,
the Merciful.

1. The Calamity!
2. What is the Calamity?
3. Ah, what will convey unto you what the Calamity is!
4. A Day wherein mankind will be as thickly-scattered moths
5. And the mountains will become as carded wool.
6. Then, as for him whose scales are heavy (with good works),
7. He will live a pleasant life.
8. But as for him whose scales are light,
9. The Bereft and Hungry One will be his mother.
10. Ah, what will convey unto you what she is!
11. Raging fire.

EXPLANATION:

101:1-5. Al-Qāri'ah, the Day of Clamor or Calamity, is the Day of Judgment. On that Day, there will be a big explosion and this physical world will come to an end. Human beings will fly like moths in the wind, and sturdy mountains will be thrown like carded wool.

101:6-11. On that Day, there will be two kinds of people, those whose good actions are heavy and those whose good actions are light. The first group will be honored with Paradise and will lead a life of ease and pleasure forever. The second group will forever suffer in the bottomless pit of a blazing Fire.

WE HAVE LEARNED:

* The Day of Judgment is a certainty.
* Even the most powerful of people will find themselves helpless on that Day.
* We must prepare ourselves in this life, so that our scale of good deeds becomes heavier and thus helps us to achieve success.

VOCABULARY

١٠١-سُورَةُ ٱلْقَارِعَةِ

١-اَلْقَارِعَةُ	*Al-Qāri'ah (tu)*	The Calamity, The Day of Noise
٢- مَا اَلْقَارِعَةُ	*Ma-(a)l-Qāri'ah(tu)*	What (is) The Calamity, the Day of Noise
٣-وَمَا أَدْرَاكَ	*Wa-mā 'adrā-ka*	will explain to you, will convey to you
مَا ٱلْقَارِعَةُ	*mā(a)l-Qāri'ah(tu)*	what the Day of Noise (is), the Calamity (is)
٤-يَوْمَ	*Yawma*	(It is) a day
يَكُونُ	*yakūnu*	will be, whereon
اَلنَّاسُ	*'an-nāsu*	humankind, men
كَٱلْفَرَاشِ	*ka-(a)l-farāshi*	like moths
اَلْمَبْثُوثِ	*'al-mabthūth(i)*	scattered about
٥-وَتَكُونُ	*Wa-takūnu*	And will be, will become
اَلْجِبَالُ	*'al-jibālu*	the mountains
كَالْعِهْنِ	*ka-(a)l-'ihn(i)*	as wool
اَلْمَنْفُوشِ	*al-manfūsh(i)*	carded
٦-فَأَمَّا	*Fa-'ammā*	Then, as for
مَنْ ثَقُلَتْ	*man thaqulat*	he whose are heavy
مَوَازِينُهُ	*mawāzinu-hū*	his balance, his scale (of deeds)
٧-فَهُوَ	*Fa-huwa*	So he
فِى	*fī*	is in
عِيشَةٍ	*'īshati(r)*	life
رَاضِيَةٍ	*rāḍiyah(tin)*	pleasant, satisfactory
٨-وَأَمَّا	*Wa-'ammā*	And, but

مَنْ	*man*	he whose
خَفَّتْ	*khaffat*	will be found light
مَوَازِينُهُ	*mawāzinu-hū*	his balance, his scales
فَأُمُّهُ	*fa-'ummu-hū*	so his home, so his mother
هَاوِيَةٌ	*hāwiyah(tun)*	in the pit, in a bottomless pit
١٠- وَمَا أدْرٰكَ	*Wa-mā 'adrā-ka*	And what will explain to you
مَا هِيَهْ	*mā hiyah*	what is this
١١-نَارٌ	*Nār(un)*	(It is) a fire
حَامِيَةٌ	*ḥāmiyah(tun)*	raging, blazing fiercely

Lesson 16

سُورَةُ العَادِيَات

AL-'ĀDIYĀT, 100:1-11

THOSE THAT RUN / THE COURSERS

Revealed in Makkah

INTRODUCTION:

This is an early Makkan *Sūrah*. It describes human love for this world and ungratefulness to Allāh (SWT). However, He is Aware of our thoughts and actions.

TRANSLITERATION:	**ARABIC TEXT:**
Bismillāhi-(a)r-Raḥmāni-(a)r-Raḥīm(i)	بِسْمِ اللّٰهِ الرَّحْمٰنِ الرَّحِيْمِ
1. *Wa-(a)l-'ādiyāti ḍabḥā(n)*	-وَالْعٰدِيٰتِ ضَبْحًا ۝
2. *Fa-(a)l-mūriyāti qadḥā(n)*	-فَالْمُوْرِيٰتِ قَدْحًا ۝
3. *Fa-(a)l-mughīrāti ṣubḥā(n)*	-فَالْمُغِيْرٰتِ صُبْحًا ۝
4. *Fa-'atharna bi-hī naq'ā(n)*	-فَأَثَرْنَ بِهٖ نَقْعًا ۝
5. *Fa-wasaṭna bi-hī jam'ā(n)*	-فَوَسَطْنَ بِهٖ جَمْعًا ۝
6. *'Inna-(a)l-'insāna li-Rabbi-hī la-kanūd(un)*	-إِنَّ الْإِنْسَانَ لِرَبِّهٖ لَكَنُوْدٌ ۝
7. *Wa 'inna-hū 'alā dhālika la-shahīd(un)*	-وَإِنَّهٗ عَلٰى ذٰلِكَ لَشَهِيْدٌ ۝
8. *Wa 'inna-hū li-ḥubbi-(a)l-khairi la-shadīd(un)*	-وَإِنَّهٗ لِحُبِّ الْخَيْرِ لَشَدِيْدٌ ۝
9. *'Afalā ya'lamu 'idhā bu'thira mā-fi-(a)l-qubūr(i)*	-أَفَلَا يَعْلَمُ إِذَا بُعْثِرَ مَا فِي الْقُبُوْرِ ۝
10. *Wa ḥuṣṣila mā fi-(a)ṣ-ṣudūr(i)*	-وَحُصِّلَ مَا فِي الصُّدُوْرِ ۝
11. *'Inna Rabba-hum bi-him yawma'idhin la-khabīr(un)*	-إِنَّ رَبَّهُمْ بِهِمْ يَوْمَئِذٍ لَّخَبِيْرٌ ۝

TRANSLATIONS:

In the name of Allāh, Most Gracious,
Most Merciful.

1. By the (Steeds) that run,
with panting (breath),
2. And strike sparks of fire,
3. And push home the charge in the morning,
4. And raise the dust in clouds the while,
5. And penetrate forthwith into
the midst (of the foe) *En masse* -
6. Truly Man is, to his Lord, ungrateful;
7. And to that (fact) he bears
witness (by his deeds);
8. And violent is he in his love of wealth.
9. Does he not know, when that which is
in the graves is scattered abroad
10. And that which is (locked up) in (human)
breasts is made manifest-
11. That their Lord had been well-acquainted
with them, (even to) that Day?

In the name of Allāh, the Beneficent,
the Merciful.

1. By the snorting
coursers,
2. Striking sparks of fire
3. And scouring to the raid at dawn.
4. Then, therewith, with their trail of dust,
5. Cleaving, as one, the center
(of the foe),
6. Lo! man is ingrate unto his Lord
7. And lo! he is a
witness unto that;
8. And lo! in love of wealth he is violent.
9. Knows he not that, when the
contents of the graves are poured forth
10. And the secrets of the
breasts are made known,
11. On that Day will their Lord be perfectly
informed concerning them.

EXPLANATION:

100:1-5. Allāh (SWT) swears by the war horses that are swift and bold. They charge into enemy ranks upon command from their masters. They obey orders and do not hesitate to risk their lives for their masters' sakes.

100:5-7. Compared with the swift, obedient horses, human beings are generally ungrateful to their Master and Lord, Allāh (SWT). Their conduct itself is a witness to their disobedience.

100:8. Ungratefulness to Allāh (SWT) is primarily caused by love for this world. Man is so busy piling up wealth, acquiring more and more of the pleasurable things in life and in gaining greater and greater influence, that he forgets his duties to his Creator.

100:9. Human beings will be brought to life again and taken out of their graves, and Allāh (SWT) will know all their actions and deeds.

100:10. On the Day of Judgment, actions will be judged; and secret thoughts, hidden plots and evil designs will be made manifest.

100:11. Allāh (SWT) knows all things. Our actions and intentions are known to Him. On the Day of Judgment, open actions and hidden intentions will be taken into account.

<u>WE HAVE LEARNED</u>:

* Many animals instinctively serve their masters and are faithful to them.
* Human beings have been given intelligence and thus have all the more reason to serve their Lord, Allāh (SWT).
* The right path of Islam leads directly to the Lord and Creator and prepares us for the Day of Judgment.

VOCABULARY

١٠٠-سُورَةُ ٱلعَادِيَاتِ

١-وَٱلْعَـٰدِيَـٰتِ	*Wa-(a)l-'ādiyāti*	By the steeds that run
ضَبْحًا	*ḍabḥa(n)*	with panting breath
٢-فَٱلْمُورِيَـٰتِ	*Fa-(a)l-mūriyāti*	And by the striking sparks
قَدْحًا	*qadḥā(n)*	sparks of fire
٣-فَٱلْمُغِيرَٰتِ	*Fa-(a)l-mughīrāti*	And by them which push home the charge
صُبْحًا	*ṣubḥā(n)*	in the morning
٤-فَأَثَرْنَ	*Fa-'atharna*	Then they raise up
بِهِ	*bi-hī*	with it
نَقْعًا	*naq'ā(n)*	the dust
٥-فَوَسَطْنَ	*Fa-wasaṭna*	And penetrate, forthwith
بِهِ	*bi-hī*	with it, by it, through it
جَمْعًا	*jam'a(n)*	*en-masse*, as one together

٦-إِنَّ	*'Inna*	Surely, Truly, Indeed
اَلإِنْسَانَ	*'al-'insāna*	Man, the humankind
لِرَبِّهِ	*li-Rabbi-hī*	to his Lord
لَكَنُودٌ	*la-kanūd(un)*	surely, ungrateful
٧-وَإِنَّهُ	*Wa-'inna-hū*	And indeed he
عَلَى ذَٰلِكَ	*'alā dhālika*	to that (fact)
لَشَهِيدٌ	*la-shahīd(un)*	He is a witness
٨-وَإِنَّهُ	*Wa-'inna-hū*	And lo he ! And indeed he
لِحُبِّ	*li-ḥubbi*	for (his) love of
اَلْخَيْرِ	*'al-khair(i)*	wealth
لَشَدِيدٌ	*la-shadīd(un)*	extreme, extravagant
٩-أَفَلاَ يَعْلَمُ	*'Afalā ya'lamu*	Does he not know
إِذَا بُعْثِرَ	*'idhā bu'thira*	when poured forth, when scattered abroad
مَا فِى	*mā fī*	that which is in, whatever is in
اَلْقُبُورِ	*'al-qubūr(i)*	the graves
١٠-وَحُصِّلَ	*Wa-ḥuṣṣila*	Are made known, is made manifest
مَا فِى	*mā fī*	that which is in , whatever is in
اَلصُّدُورِ	*'aṣ-ṣudūr(i)*	the breasts
١١-إِنَّ	*'Inna*	Indeed, surely
رَبَّهُمْ	*Rabba-hum*	their Lord
بِهِمْ	*bi-him*	with them, concerning them
يَوْمَئِذٍ	*yawma'idhin*	on that day
لَخَبِيرٌ	*la-khabīr(un)*	surely is informed, is perfectly informed

Lesson 17

سورة الزلزلة

AZ-ZALZALAH, 99:1-8

THE EARTHQUAKE / THE EARTHQUAKE

Revealed in Madīnah

INTRODUCTION:

This *Sūrah* is generally regarded as belonging to the early Madinah period, but it could be late Makkan as well. In general, this *Sūrah* deals with the predominant Makkan theme of the Day of Judgment, its horrors and its system of perfect justice.

TRANSLITERATION:	**ARABIC TEXT:**
Bismillāhi-(a)r-Raḥmāni-(a)r-Raḥīm(i)	بِسْمِ اللّٰهِ الرَّحْمٰنِ الرَّحِيْمِ
1. *'Idhā zulzilati-(a)l-'arḍu zilzāla-hā*	إِذَا زُلْزِلَتِ الْأَرْضُ زِلْزَالَهَا ۝
2. *Wa 'akhrajati-(a)l-'arḍu 'athqāla-hā*	وَأَخْرَجَتِ الْأَرْضُ أَثْقَالَهَا ۝
3. *Wa qāla-(a)l-'insānu mā-la-hā*	وَقَالَ الْإِنْسَانُ مَا لَهَا ۝
4. *Yawma'idhin tuḥaddithu 'akhbāra-hā*	يَوْمَئِذٍ تُحَدِّثُ أَخْبَارَهَا ۝
5. *Bi 'anna Rabba-ka 'awḥā-la-hā*	بِأَنَّ رَبَّكَ أَوْحَىٰ لَهَا ۝
6. *Yawma'idhin yaṣduru-(a)n-nāsu 'ashtātal-*	يَوْمَئِذٍ يَصْدُرُ النَّاسُ أَشْتَاتًا
li-yuraw 'a'māla-hum	لِيُرَوْا أَعْمَالَهُمْ ۝
7. *Fa-man ya'mal mithqāla dharratin khairan yarah(u)*	فَمَنْ يَعْمَلْ مِثْقَالَ ذَرَّةٍ خَيْرًا يَرَهُ ۝
8. *Wa man ya'mal mithqāla dharatin sharran yarah(u)*	وَمَنْ يَعْمَلْ مِثْقَالَ ذَرَّةٍ شَرًّا يَرَهُ ۝

TRANSLATIONS:

In the name of Allāh, Most Gracious,
Most Merciful.

1. When the Earth is shaken
to her (utmost) convulsion,
2. And the Earth throws up
its burdens (from within),
3. And man cries (distressed):
what is the matter with it?
4. On that Day will it declare its tidings:
5. For that your Lord will
have given its inspiration.
6. On that Day will men proceed in companies
sorted out, to be shown
the deeds that they (had done)
7. Then shall anyone who has done
an atom's weight of good, see it!
8. And anyone who has done
an atom's weight of evil, shall see it.

In the name of Allāh, the Beneficent,
the Merciful.

1. When Earth is shaken
with her (final) earthquake
2. And Earth yields up
her burdens,
3. And man says:
What ails her?
4. That Day she will relate her chronicles.
5. Because your Lord
inspired her.
6. That Day mankind will issue forth in sorted
scattered groups to be shown
their deeds.
7. And whoso does good an
atom's weight will see it then,
8. And whoso does
ill an atom's weight will see it then.

EXPLANATION:

99:1-2. On the Last Day, the world will undergo a terrible earthquake. It will throw off whatever it had contained within itself: human beings it had held as a trust, rich minerals and volcanic fires.

99:3. This terrifying experience will be more terrible than any that human beings have ever seen or experienced. The Day of Judgment will catch everyone by surprise and Mankind will ask one another: "What is happening?"

99:4-5. On that Day, Allāh (SWT) will inspire the Earth to speak. It will report every individual's actions, good or bad.

MOTHER EARTH

Rasūlullāh (S) has said: "Be careful of Earth; it is your mother. There is no one on earth doing good or bad that it does not know about."

99:6. All people will be sorted and put into groups, the righteous and the evil-doers, according to their actions.

99:7-8. People will be able to view all their actions, even hidden motives and intentions will be made known to them. There will be reward or punishment for even the smallest of actions.
The Believers can hope for Allāh's Mercy and the shafā'ah (intercession) of Rasūlullāh (S).

WE HAVE LEARNED:

* The Day of Judgment is a certainty, and it will be heralded by violent eruptions.
* On that Day, human beings will be rewarded or punished according to their actions.
* The time is now to prepare for that Day.

VOCABULARY

٩٩-سُورَةُ ٱلزَّلْزَلَة

١-إذا	*'Idhā*	When
زُلْزِلَت	*zulzilati*	is shaken
اَلأَرْضُ	*'al-'arḍu*	the Earth
زِلْزالَها	*zilzāla-hā*	to her utmost shaking, convulsion
٢-وأَخْرَجَتِ	*Wa-'akhrajat(i)*	And throws up, yields up
اَلأَرْضُ	*'al-'arḍ(u)*	the Earth
أثقالَها	*'athqāla-hā*	her burdens
٣-وقَالَ	*Wa-qāla*	And will say (said)
اَلإِنْسانُ	*'al-'insānu*	Man, humankind
ما لَها	*mā la-hā*	what is (the matter) with her
٤-يَومَئِذٍ	*Yawma'idhin*	On that day
تُحَدِّثُ	*tuḥaddithu*	will relate, will declare
أَخْبارَها	*'akhbāra-hā*	her chronicles, her tidings

٥-بِأَنَّ	*Bi-'anna*	For that
رَبَّكَ	*Rabba-ka*	your Lord
أَوْحَىٰ	*'aw-ḥā*	inspired, has given inspiration
لَهَا	*la-hā*	to her
٦-يَوْمَئِذٍ	*Yawma'idhin*	On that day
يَصْدُرُ	*yaṣduru*	will issue forth
اَلنَّاسُ	*'an-nāsu*	the Men, the humankind
أَشْتَاتًا	*'ashtāt(an)*	in scattered groups
لِيُرَوْا	*li-yuraw*	to be shown
أَعْمَـٰلَهُمْ	*'a'māla-hum*	their deeds
٧-فَمَنْ	*Fa-man*	As for who
يَعْمَلْ	*ya'mal*	has done
مِثقَالَ	*mithqāla*	equal in weight
ذَرَّةٍ	*dharrat(in)*	atom
خَيراً	*khairan*	of good
يَرَهُ	*yara-h(u)*	will see it
٨-وَمَنْ	*Wa-man*	As for him
يَعْمَلْ	*ya'mal*	has done
مِثْقَالَ	*mithqāla*	equal in weight
ذَرَّةٍ	*dharrat(in)*	atom
شَرًّا	*sharr(an)*	of evil, ill
يَرَهُ	*yara-h(u)*	he will see it

Lesson 18 سُورَةُ البَيِّنَة

AL-BAYYINAH, 98:1-8

THE CLEAR EVIDENCE / THE CLEAR PROOF

Revealed in Madīnah

INTRODUCTION:

This is an early Madīnah *Sūrah*. It deals with the negative attitude of the People of the Book, the Jews and the Christians, to the mission of Rasūlullāh (S). It divides humanity into two groups: the believers who are worthy of Allāh's pleasure, and the non-believers who deserve the punishment of Allāh (SWT) for their disobedience. This division of humanity is not based on race, language or origin, but rather on faith and actions.

TRANSLITERATION:	**ARABIC TEXT:**
Bismillāhi-(a)r-Raḥmāni-(a)r-Raḥīm(i)	بِسْمِ اللَّهِ الرَّحْمَٰنِ الرَّحِيمِ
1. *Lam yakuni-(a)l-ladhīna kafarū min 'ahli-(a)l-kitābi*	-لَمْ يَكُنِ الَّذِينَ كَفَرُوا مِنْ أَهْلِ الْكِتَابِ
wa-(a)l-mushrikīna munfakkīna	وَالْمُشْرِكِينَ مُنفَكِّينَ
ḥattā ta'tiya humu-(a)l-bayyinah(tu)	حَتَّىٰ تَأْتِيَهُمُ الْبَيِّنَةُ ۝
2. *Rasūlun min-Allāhi yatlū ṣuḥufan muṭahharah(tan)*	-رَسُولٌ مِّنَ اللَّهِ يَتْلُو صُحُفًا مُّطَهَّرَةً ۝
3. *Fī-hā kutubun qayyimah(tun)*	-فِيهَا كُتُبٌ قَيِّمَةٌ ۝
4. *Wa mā tafarraqa-(a)l-ladhīna 'ūtu-(a)l-kitāba 'illā*	-وَمَا تَفَرَّقَ الَّذِينَ أُوتُوا الْكِتَابَ إِلَّا
min ba'di mā jā'at humu-(a)l-bayyinah(tu)	مِن بَعْدِ مَا جَاءَتْهُمُ الْبَيِّنَةُ ۝
5. *Wa mā 'umirū 'illā li-ya' budū-(A)llāha mukhliṣīna*	-وَمَا أُمِرُوا إِلَّا لِيَعْبُدُوا اللَّهَ مُخْلِصِينَ
lahu-d-dīna ḥunafā'a wa yuqīmū-(a)ṣ-ṣalāta	لَهُ الدِّينَ حُنَفَاءَ وَيُقِيمُوا الصَّلَاةَ
wa yu'tu-(a)z-zakāta wa dhālika dīnu-(a)l-qayyimah(ti)	وَيُؤْتُوا الزَّكَاةَ وَذَٰلِكَ دِينُ الْقَيِّمَةِ ۝

6. 'Inna-(a)l-ladhīna kafarū min 'ahli-(a)l-kitābi

   wa-(a)l-mushrikīna fī nāri jahannama khālidīna fī-hā

   ulā'ika hum sharru-(a)l-bariyyah(ti)

اِنَّ الَّذِيْنَ كَفَرُوْا مِنْ اَهْلِ الْكِتٰبِ
وَالْمُشْرِكِيْنَ فِيْ نَارِ جَهَنَّمَ خٰلِدِيْنَ فِيْهَا ۚ
اُولٰٓئِكَ هُمْ شَرُّ الْبَرِيَّةِ ۗ

7. 'Inna-(a)l-ladhīna 'āmanu wa 'amilu-(a)s-sāliḥāti

   'ulā'ika hum khairu-(a)l-bariyyah(ti)

اِنَّ الَّذِيْنَ اٰمَنُوْا وَعَمِلُوا الصّٰلِحٰتِ
اُولٰٓئِكَ هُمْ خَيْرُ الْبَرِيَّةِ ۗ

8. Jazā'u-hum 'inda Rabbi-him jannātu 'adnin

   tajrī min taḥti-ha-(a)l-'anhāru

   khālidīna fī-hā 'abada Raḍiya-Allāhu 'an-hum

   wa raḍū 'an-hu dhālika li-man khashiya Rabbah(u)

جَزَآؤُهُمْ عِنْدَ رَبِّهِمْ جَنّٰتُ عَدْنٍ
تَجْرِيْ مِنْ تَحْتِهَا الْاَنْهٰرُ
خٰلِدِيْنَ فِيْهَآ اَبَدًا ۚ رَضِيَ اللّٰهُ عَنْهُمْ
وَرَضُوْا عَنْهُ ۗ ذٰلِكَ لِمَنْ خَشِيَ رَبَّهٗ ۗ

TRANSLATIONS:

In the name of Allāh, Most Gracious,
Most Merciful.

1. Those who reject (Truth), among the
   People of the Book and among the Polytheists,
   were not going to depart (from their ways) until
   there should come to them Clear Evidence,
2. A Messenger from Allāh,
   rehearsing scriptures kept pure and holy;
3. In which are laws right and straight.
4. Nor did the People of the Book,
   make schisms until after there
   came to them Clear Evidence.
5. And they have been commanded no more
   than this: to worship Allāh, offering Him
   sincere devotion, being True (in faith);
   to establish regular Prayer;
   and to practice regular Charity;
   and that is the Religion Right and Straight.

In the name of Allāh, the Beneficent,
the Merciful.

1. Those who disbelieve among the
   People of the Scripture and the idolaters
   could not have left off (erring) till
   the clear proof came unto them,
2. A messenger from Allāh, reading
   purified pages,
3. Containing correct scriptures.
4. Nor were the People of the Scripture
   divided until after the
   clear proof came unto them.
5. And they are ordained naught else
   than to serve Allāh, keeping religion
   pure for Him, as men by nature upright
   and to establish worship
   and to pay the poor-due.
   That is true religion.

6. Those who reject (Truth), among the People of the Book and among the Polytheists, will be in hell-fire, to dwell in it (for ever). They are the worst of creatures.
7. Those who have faith and do righteous deeds, they are the best of creatures.
8. Their reward is with Allāh: Gardens of Eternity, beneath which rivers flow; they will dwell in them forever; Allāh well pleased with them, and they with Him: All this for such as fear their Lord and Cherisher.

6. Lo! those who disbelieve, among the People of the Scripture and idolaters, will abide in fire of hell. They are worst of created beings.
7. (And) lo! those who believe and do good works are the best of created beings.
8. Their reward is with their Lord: Gardens of Eden underneath which rivers flow, wherein they dwell for ever. Allāh has pleasure in them and they have pleasure in Him This is (in store) for him who fears his Lord.

EXPLANATION:

98:1-2. The People of the Book and the *mushrikūn* (polytheists) were erring in their ways during this period. They were in need of a clear message for their guidance. Allāh (SWT) decided to send His Messenger with the Holy Qur'ān. This message is written down clearly, in various chapters *(Suwar)*.

98:3-5. The People of the Book had received Allāh's clear instruction through His earlier Revelations. They were enjoined the same message of sincerely worshipping Allāh (SWT), keeping His religion pure from any *shirk* (accepting partners with Allāh), remaining upright in His path, establishing the *Salāh* and paying the *Zakāh*. This in fact, is the basis of true religion of Allāh (SWT). These fundamentals are the core of the Islamic message, sent down for all peoples of this world. It came in its final form through Rasūlullāh (S), and is now contained within the Qur'ān.

98:6. The People of the Book had no excuse for refuting the message of Islam. They had received the message through the earlier prophets, and now Rasūlullāh (S) had come to them with the same clear evidence from Allāh (SWT). For the *mushrikūn*, also, there was no excuse. Rasūlullāh (S) was from amongst their own. He spoke the same language that they did, and brought a clear message for them. Both the People of the Book and the *mushrikūn* will be punished for their denial and disobedience.

98:7-8. The believers, in contrast, are the best among human beings; worthy of *Jannah* and the many pleasures of the Hereafter.

It must, however, be noted that the believers were not a specific ethnic group; but consisted of former *kuffār, mushrikūn* and the People of the Book who accepted Islam and recognized the clear evidence of the Qur'ān that Rasūlullāh (S) brought for the people.

WE HAVE LEARNED:

* The message of the Qur'ān and the life of Rasūlullāh (S) offers clear evidence of the truth for everyone to see for themselves.
* The doors of Islam are always open for every seeker of the Truth.
* There is no excuse for anyone to deny the Truth after clear guidance has come to them.

VOCABULARY

٩٨- سُورَةُ ٱلبَيِّنَةِ

١- لَم يَكُنِ	*Lam yakun(i)*	Were not, could not have
ٱلَّذِينَ	*'alladhīna*	those who
كَفَرُوا	*kafarū*	disbelieved, rejected faith
مِنْ	*min*	from among
أَهْلِ ٱلْكِتَـٰبِ	*'ahli-(a)l-kitāb(i)*	the People of the Book
وَٱلْمُشْرِكِينَ	*wa-(a)l-mushrikīna*	and the idolators
مُنْفَكِّينَ	*munfakkīna*	going to depart, have left off
حَتَّىٰ	*ḥatta*	until, till
تَأْتِيَهُمُ	*ta'tiya-humu*	should come to them
ٱلْبَيِّنَةُ	*'al-bayyinah(tu)*	the Clear Proof, the Clear Evidence
٢-رَسُولٌ	*Rasūl(un)*	A Messenger
مِّنَ ٱللَّهِ	*min 'Allāh(i)*	from Allah
يَتْلُوا صُحُفًا	*yatlū ṣuḥufan*	reading pages, rehearsing scriptures
مُّطَهَّرَةً	*muṭahharah(tan)*	purified, holy

٣-فِيهَا	*Fī-hā*	In it, wherein (are)
كُتُبٌ قَيِّمَةٌ	*kutubun qayyimah(tun)*	correct scriptures, right, decrees
٤- وَمَا تَفَرَّقَ	*Wa-mā tafarraqa*	Nor have those become divided
الَّذِينَ	*'allad͟hīna*	those who
أُوتُوا ٱلْكِتَٰبَ	*'ūtu-(a)l-kitāba*	were given the Book
إِلاَّ مِن بَعْدِ	*'illā min ba'di*	until after
مَا جَآءَتهُمُ	*mā jā'at-hum(u)*	what has come to them
الْبَيِّنَةُ	*'al-bayyinah(tu)*	the Clear Proof
٥-وَمَا أُمِرُوا	*Wa-mā 'umirū*	And they were not ordered
إِلاَّ لِيَعْبُدُوا ٱللَّهَ	*'illa li-ya'budu-(A)llāha*	no more than to worship Allah
مُخْلِصِينَ	*muk͟hliṣīna*	offering sincere devotion
لَهُ ٱلدِّينَ	*la-hu-(a)'d-dīna*	to Him keeping the religion, the faith
حُنَفَاءَ	*ḥunafā'a*	being true in faith, upright in nature
وَيُقِيمُوا	*wa-yuqīmū*	and establish
الصَّلَوٰةَ	*'aṣ-ṣalāt(a)*	the regular prayer
وَيُؤْتُوا	*wa-yu'tū*	and paying
الزَّكَوٰةَ	*'az-zakāt(a)*	the *Zakah*, the poor due
وَذَٰلِكَ	*wa-d͟hālika*	and that (is)
دِينُ ٱلْقَيِّمَةِ	*dīnu-'(a)l-qayyimah(ti)*	the religion of right and straight
٦- إِنَّ ٱلَّذِينَ	*'Inna '(a)llad͟hīna*	Indeed, those who
كَفَرُوا	*kafarū*	rejected the Truth, disbelieved
مِنْ أَهْلِ ٱلْكِتَٰبِ	*min 'ahli-(a)l-kitābi*	from among the people (of) the book
وَٱلْمُشْرِكِيْنَ	*wa-(a)l-mus͟hrikīna*	and the idolators

فِي نَارِ جَهَنَّمَ	*fī nāri Jahannama*	in fire (of) Hell
خَٰلِدِينَ فِيهَا	*khalidīna fī-hā*	dwell forever in it, to abide forever in it
أُولَٰئِكَ هُمْ	*'ulā'ika hum*	those are the
شَرُّ ٱلْبَرِيَّةِ	*sharru-(a)l-bariyyah(ti)*	worst of beings, most evil (of) creatures
٧- إِنَّ ٱلَّذِينَ	*'Inna 'alladhīna*	Surely those who
ءَامَنُوا وَعَمِلُوا	*'āmanū wa-'amilū*	believed and did, had faith and do
اَلصَّٰلِحَٰتِ	*'aṣ-ṣāliḥāti*	good deeds, righteous deeds
أُولَٰئِكَ هُمْ	*'ulā'ikahum*	those they are
خَيْرُ ٱلْبَرِيَّةِ	*khairu-(a)l-bariyyah(ti)*	the best (of) creatures
٨-جَزَآؤُهُمْ	*Jazā'u-hum*	Their Reward (is)
عِنْدَ رَبِّهِمْ	*'inda Rabbi-him*	with their Lord
جَنَّٰتُ عَدْنٍ	*Jannātu 'Adnin*	Gardens (of) Eternity, Gardens of Eden
تَجْرِى	*tajrī*	flow
مِن تَحْتِهَا	*min taḥti-hā*	from underneath it, from beneath it
اَلأَنْهَٰرُ	*'al-'anhāru*	the rivers
خَٰلِدِينَ	*khālidīna*	abiding forever
فِيهَا أَبَداً	*fī-hā 'abada(n)*	in them, therein forever
رَضِىَ ٱللَّهُ	*raḍiya-(A)llāhu*	Allah is pleased
عَنْهُمْ	*'an-hum*	with them
وَرَضُوا عَنْهُ	*wa-raḍū 'an-Hu*	and they are pleased with Him
ذَٰلِكَ لِمَنْ	*dhālika li-man*	such is, (the reward) for him who
خَشِىَ رَبَّهُ	*khashiya Rabba-h(u)*	fears his Lord

Lesson 19

سُورَةُ القَدْرِ

AL-QADR, 97:1-5

THE NIGHT OF POWER (OR HONOR) / POWER

Revealed in Makkah

INTRODUCTION:

This is a Makkan *Sūrah.* It describes the greatness of the *Lailat-u-(A)l-Qadr*, the Night of Power. The Qur'ān was revealed during this blessed night and Allāh (SWT) has made it a special time for the believers to seek His Mercy and Favor. *Lailat-u-(A)l-Qadr* is found in the last ten nights of Ramadān, the month of fasting.

TRANSLITERATION:

Bismillāhi-(a)r-Rahmāni-(a)r-Rahīm(i)

1. *'Inna 'anzalnā-hu fī Lailat-i-(a)l-Qadr(i)*
2. *Wa mā 'adrā-ka mā Lailatu-(a)l-Qadr(i)*
3. *Lailatu-(a)l-Qadri khairun min 'alfi shahr(in)*
4. *Tanazzalu-(a)l-malā'ikatu wa-(a)r-Rūhu*
   fī-hā bi'idhni Rabbi-him min kulli 'amr(in)
5. *Salām(un) hiya hattā matla'i-(a)l-Fajr(i)*

ARABIC TEXT:

بِسْمِ اللهِ الرَّحْمٰنِ الرَّحِيْمِ

-إِنَّآ أَنزَلْنَٰهُ فِى لَيْلَةِ ٱلْقَدْرِ ۝

-وَمَآ أَدْرَىٰكَ مَا لَيْلَةُ ٱلْقَدْرِ ۝

-لَيْلَةُ ٱلْقَدْرِ خَيْرٌ مِّنْ أَلْفِ شَهْرٍ ۝

-تَنَزَّلُ ٱلْمَلَٰٓئِكَةُ وَٱلرُّوحُ

فِيهَا بِإِذْنِ رَبِّهِم مِّن كُلِّ أَمْرٍ ۝

-سَلَٰمٌ هِىَ حَتَّىٰ مَطْلَعِ ٱلْفَجْرِ ۝

TRANSLATIONS:

In the name of Allāh, Most Gracious,
Most Merciful.

1. We have indeed revealed this (Message) in the Night of Power.

In the name of Allāh, the Beneficent,
the Merciful.

1. Lo! We revealed it on the Night of Power.

2. And what will explain to you
   what the Night of Power is?
3. The Night of Power is better
   than a thousand months.
4. In it come down the angels and the Spirit
   by Allāh's permission,
   on every errand:
5. Peace! This until
   the rise of Morn.

2. Ah, what will convey unto you
   what the Night of Power is!
3. The Night of Power is better
   than a thousand months.
4. The angels and the Spirit descend therein,
   by the permission of their Lord,
   with all decrees.
5. (That night is) peace until
   the rising of the dawn.

EXPLANATION:

97:1-2. *Lailat-ul-Qadr* is the Night of Power, the night in which the Qur'ān was revealed. The Arabic term *Qadr* has two meanings: power and greatness, and decision making. This night contains special blessings and greatness because it was the night during which the Qur'ān was revealed to Rasūlullāh (S). On this night, Allāh (SWT) makes decisions about the coming year; and Jibrīl (A) and the other Angels carry these decisions to the world on this night.

97:3. It is a night of special blessings. It contains more blessings than can be found in one thousand months. Mujāhid (R) once said: "Any good deed, fasting (during the day), and prayers, are better than if these same actions are performed for one thousand months."

One thousand months are calculated to be equal to eighty three years and four months; the average life-span of a human being. The number one thousand, however, must not be taken too literally. It is used as a figure of speech, to make us understand the great significance of this night. In fact, no one can really calculate the blessings of this night.

Rasūlullāh (S) has said to seek this night in the last ten nights of Ramaḍān. In another place, he asked us to seek it in the odd nights of the last ten days. And yet another time, he pointed out to the night of the twenty-seventh as being the night. These varying statements suggest that Allāh (SWT) wants us to seek it in the last ten days of Ramaḍān, and to offer special prayers and do good deeds and receive a special reward for these good actions.

97:4-5. The Angels descend during this Blessed Night with special orders from Allāh (SWT). This is a "Night of Peace", until dawn arrives.

WE HAVE LEARNED:

* The Qur'ān was revealed in the month of Ramadan on the Night of Power.
* Worship and charity in the Night of Power is better than the worship of one thousand months.
* We should seek *Lailat ul-Qadr* in the last ten days of Ramadan.

A SPECIAL FAVOR

Rasūlullāh (S) learned about a Mujāhid from one of the early *'Umam,* who continuously struggled in the way of Allāh (SWT) for one thousand months. When Rasūlullāh (S) and his *Saḥābah* heard this story they greatly appreciated it. Rasūlullāh (S) realized that the average age of his own *'Ummah* is much shorter now than it had been for the earlier people. He desired the same opportunity for his *'Ummah* to struggle in the way of Allāh (SWT). Therefore, he said to Him: "People of my *'Ummah* have the shortest life, and they can perform the fewest of the good deeds."

Allāh (SWT) accepted the prayers of Rasūlullāh (S) and gave his *'Ummah Lailat ul-Qadr*, as a special blessing. The month of Ramadān and *Lailat ul-Qadr* are special times created by Allāh, to bring the believers closer to Him. We must take full advantage of this gift from Allāh (SWT).

VOCABULARY

٩٧- سُورَةُ ٱلْقَدْرِ

١- إِنَّآ أَنزَلْنَٰهُ	*'Inna 'anzalnā-hu*	Indeed! We have revealed it
فِى لَيْلَةِ الْقَدْرِ	*fī Lailati-(a)l-Qadr(i)*	in the Night of Power
٢- وَمَآ أَدْرَٰكَ	*Wa-mā 'adrā-ka*	And what will explain to you
مَا لَيْلَةُ ٱلْقَدْرِ	*mā Lailatu-(a)l-Qadr(i)*	what is the Night of Power
٣-لَيْلَةُ الْقَدْرِ	*Lailatu-(a)l-Qadri*	the Night of Power
خَيْرٌ مِّنْ	*khairun min*	(is) better than
أَلْفِ شَهْرٍ	*'alfi shahr(in)*	a thousand months

٤-تَنَزَّلُ	*Tanazzalu*	Descend, come down
اَلْمَلَٰئِكَةُ	*'al-malā'ikatu*	the angels
وَٱلرُّوحُ	*wa-(a)r-Rūḥu*	and the Spirit
فِيهَا	*fī-hā*	in it
بِإِذْنِ رَبِّهِمْ	*bi-'idhni Rabbi-him*	by permission of their Lord
مِّنْ كُلِّ	*min kulli*	on, every
أَمْرٍ	*'amr(in)*	errand, decree
٥-سَلَٰمٌ	*Salām(un)*	Peace
هِيَ حَتَّىٰ	*hiya ḥattā*	it is until, till
مَطْلَعِ ٱلْفَجْرِ	*maṭla'i-(a)l-fajr(i)*	rising of the morning, the dawn

سُورَةُ الْعَلَقِ

Lesson 20

AL-'ALAQ, OR'IQRA', 96:1-19

THE CLINGING CLOT, OR READ / READ

Revealed in Makkah

INTRODUCTION:

This *Sūrah* was revealed in two parts. The first part, verses 1-5, was the first Revelation to Rasūlullāh (S), as he sat in the cave of *Ḥirā'*. The second part, verses 6-19, was revealed a little later, when the news of Rasūlullāh's Prophethood reached the Makkans, and the *kuffār* opposition began to grow.

It has been related that Rasūlullāh (S) was sitting in the cave of *Ḥirā'* when Angel Jibrīl (A) came to him and commanded him, "Read!" However, Rasūlullāh (S) did not know how to read or write. Thus, he replied, "I do not know how to read or write." Angel Jibrīl (A) embraced him tightly and repeated, "Read!" Rasūlullāh (S) gave the same reply. The Angel embraced him a second time, and again commanded him to "Read!"

Rasūlullāh's heart opened to receive Allāh's First Revelation. He was able to follow the Angel and recite after him the first five verses of this *Sūrah.*

The second part speaks about those who had rejected the faith, and were not prepared to worship only one God.

TRANSLITERATION:	**ARABIC TEXT:**
Bismillāhi-(a)r-Raḥmāni-(a)r-Raḥīm(i)	بِسْمِ اللّٰهِ الرَّحْمٰنِ الرَّحِيْمِ
1. *'Iqra' bismi Rabbi-ka-(a)l-ladhī khalaq(a)*	اِقْرَاْ بِاسْمِ رَبِّكَ الَّذِیْ خَلَقَ ۝
2. *Khalaqa-(a)l-'insāna min 'alaq(in)*	خَلَقَ الْاِنْسَانَ مِنْ عَلَقٍ ۝
3. *'Iqra' wa Rabbu-ka-(a)l-'akram(u)*	اِقْرَاْ وَرَبُّكَ الْاَكْرَمُ ۝
4. *'Alladhī 'allama bi-(a)l-qalam(i)*	الَّذِیْ عَلَّمَ بِالْقَلَمِ ۝
5. *'Allama-(a)l-'insāna mā lam-ya'lam*	عَلَّمَ الْاِنْسَانَ مَا لَمْ یَعْلَمْ ۝

6. *Kallā 'inna-(a)l-'insāna la-yaṭghā*	كَلَّآ إِنَّ الْإِنسَانَ لَيَطْغَىٰٓ ۝
7. *'A(n)r-ra'ā-hu-(i)staghnā*	أَن رَّآهُ اسْتَغْنَىٰٓ ۝
8. *'Inna 'ilā Rabbi-ka-(a)r-ruj'ā*	إِنَّ إِلَىٰ رَبِّكَ الرُّجْعَىٰٓ ۝
9. *'Ara'aita-(a)l-ladhī yanhā*	أَرَءَيْتَ الَّذِي يَنْهَىٰ ۝
10. *'Abdan 'idhā ṣallā*	عَبْدًا إِذَا صَلَّىٰٓ ۝
11. *'Ara'aita 'in kāna 'ala-(a)l-hudā*	أَرَءَيْتَ إِن كَانَ عَلَى الْهُدَىٰٓ ۝
12. *'Aw 'amara bi-(a)t-taqwā*	أَوْ أَمَرَ بِالتَّقْوَىٰٓ ۝
13. *'A ra'aita in kadhdhaba wa tawallā*	أَرَءَيْتَ إِن كَذَّبَ وَتَوَلَّىٰٓ ۝
14. *'A lam ya'lam bi 'anna-(A)llāha yarā*	أَلَمْ يَعْلَم بِأَنَّ اللَّهَ يَرَىٰ ۝
15. *Kallā-la'il lam-yantahī lanasfa'am bi-(a)n-nāṣiyah(ti)*	كَلَّا لَئِن لَّمْ يَنتَهِ لَنَسْفَعًۢا بِالنَّاصِيَةِ ۝
16. *Nāṣiyatin kādhibatin khāṭi'ah(tin)*	نَاصِيَةٍ كَاذِبَةٍ خَاطِئَةٍ ۝
17. *Fal-yad'u nādiyah(u)*	فَلْيَدْعُ نَادِيَهُۥ ۝
18. *Sanad'u-(a)z-zabāniyah(ta)*	سَنَدْعُ الزَّبَانِيَةَ ۝
19. *Kallā-lā tuṭi'-hu wa-(a)sjud wa-(a)qtarib*	كَلَّا لَا تُطِعْهُ وَاسْجُدْ وَاقْتَرِب ۝

TRANSLATIONS:

In the name of Allāh, Most Gracious,
Most Merciful.

1. Proclaim! (or Read!) in the name of thy Lord and Cherisher, Who created-
2. Created man, out of a (mere) clot of congealed blood:
3. Proclaim! And thy Lord is the Most Bountiful,

In the name of Allāh, the Beneficent,
the Merciful.

1. Read: In the name of thy Lord who created.
2. Created man from a clot.
3. Read: And your Lord is the Most Bounteous,

4. He who taught (The use of) the Pen,	4. Who taught by the pen,
5. Taught man that which he knew not.	5. Taught man that which he knew not.
6. Nay, but man does transgress all bounds,	6. Nay, but verily man is rebellious.
7. In that he looketh upon himself as self-sufficient.	7. That he thinketh himself independent!
8. Verily, to your Lord is the return (of all).	8. Lo! unto your Lord is the return.
9. Do you see one who forbids,	9. Have you seen him who dissuadeth
10. A votary when he (turns) to pray?	10. A slave when he prayeth?
11. Do you see it he is on (the road of) Guidance?	11. Have you seen if he (relies) on the guidance (of Allāh)
12. Or enjoins Righteousness?	12. Or enjoineth piety?
13. Do you see if he denies (Truth) and turns away?	13. Have you seen if he denies (Allāh's guidance) and is froward?
14. Does he not know that Allāh does see?	14. Is he then unaware that Allāh sees?
15. Let him beware! If he desist not, We will drag him by the forelock,	15. Nay, but if he cease not, We will seize him by the forelock-
16. A lying, sinful forelock	16. The lying, sinful forelock-
17. Then, let him call (for help) to his council (of comrades):	17. Then let him call upon his henchmen!
18. We will call on the angels of punishment (to deal with him)!	18. We will call the guards of hell.
19. No, heed him not: but bow down in adoration, and bring yourself closer (to Allāh).	19. Nay! Obey not you him. But prostrate yourself, and draw near (unto Allāh).

EXPLANATION:

96:1. The first Revelation to Rasūlullāh (S) enjoins him to "Read!" (*Iqra'*). The Arabic term *Iqra'* means "read" or "proclaim." In this case, the term refers specifically to reading of the Qur'ān, which may be literally translated as "Readings" or "Proclamations." By extension, the term *Iqra'* also refers to the general reading of knowledge, which is extolled in the following verses.

96:2. Allāh (SWT) is the only *Rabb,* Who creates, supports, and sustains; and unto Him is our final return. He is One; there is no lord or god besides Him. Human beings are His best Creation, *'Ashraf al-Makhlūqāt,* but they have been created from an almost invisible clot of blood. They have been instilled with a great

96:3-4. Allāh (SWT) is the generous Lord. He has created human beings with a special potential for learning and achievement. One of His greatest blessings is the knowledge He has given us. With the beginning of formal writing and documentation, human knowledge and wisdom had been preserved for generations to come. New generations have the opportunity to build on the knowledge accumulated from the past.

96:5. Human beings have been instilled with a natural curiosity to discover the unknown. Man's thirst for knowledge is never satisfied.

96:6-8. These verses speak about human psychology in general and the attitude of the Quraish chiefs in particular. Allāh (SWT) has given human beings the freedom to choose between good and evil. Man's potential to achieve great things often makes him forgetful of Allāh (SWT) as the real cause of his success. He forgets his ultimate return to his Lord and Master on the Day of Judgment.

96:9-10. 'Abū Jahl, one of the greatest enemies of Islam, and his companions used to try to prevent Rasūlullāh (S) and the Muslims from praying at the *Ḥaram* in Makkah. From the earliest days of Rasūlūllah's mission, freedom of worship had been denied to the Muslims.

96:11-14. Allāh (SWT) watches over everyone (v. 14). He has blessed us with the ability to judge a person's character. There are three impartial criteria used to judge any man's character:

1. Has he received authorative guidance from Allāh (SWT)?
2. Does he enjoin righteousness upon others?
3. Does he deny the Truth and invent lies; does he accept the Truth, or turn his back upon it?

The characters of Rasūlullāh (S) and his opponents must be judged upon this basis.

96:15-16. Allāh (SWT) issues a warning to 'Abū Jahl and his companions to desist, or face the consequences of their evil actions. On the Day of Judgment, 'Abū Jahl will be dragged by his forelock. A forelock represents a man's honor; to be dragged by it symbolizes extreme humiliation.

96:17-18. The sinner will lack friends and supporters when the punishment of Allāh (SWT) is meted out to him.

96:19. The Messenger and his supporters were commanded not to fear the evil ones, and to turn to Allāh, Who is the only One worthy of worship. A believer must completely submit to His Will, and strive to become closer to his Lord. The Arabic term *Sajdah*, or prostration, is a position of complete surrender, as well as being one in which a believer is closest to Allāh (SWT). This is an *'āyah* of *sajdah*, and after reading it, it is obligatory to literally prostrate, as a symbol of acceptance of Allāh's Command.

WE HAVE LEARNED:

* Allāh (SWT) has enjoined all of us to read and acquire knowledge.
* The *kuffār* are warned of the evil consequences of their opposition and disbelief.
* The Believers are advised to ignore the opposition and strive to be closer to Allāh (SWT).

VOCABULARY

٩٦-سُورَةُ ٱلعَلَق

١-اقْرَأْ	*'Iqra'*	Read, proclaim
بِٱسْمِ رَبِّكَ	*bi-(i)s-mi Rabbi-ka*	in the name of your Lord
ٱلَّذِى خَلَقَ	*'Alladhī khalaq(a)*	Who created
٢-خَلَقَ ٱلإِنْسَٰنَ	*khalaqa-(a)l-'insāna*	Created Man, human beings
مِنْ عَلَقٍ	*min 'alaq(in)*	from clot of congealed blood
٣-اقْرَأْ	*'Iqra'*	Read, proclaim
وَرَبُّكَ ٱلأَكْرَمُ	*wa-Rabbu-ka-(a)l-'Akram(u)*	and your Lord is Most Bounteous
٤-ٱلَّذِى	*'Alladhī*	That He Who
عَلَّمَ بِٱلقَلَمِ	*'allama bi-(a)l-qalam(i)*	Taught (the use of) pen
٥-عَلَّمَ ٱلإِنسَٰنَ	*'Allama-(a)l-'insāna*	Taught Man
مَا لَمْ يَعْلَمْ	*ma lam-ya'lam*	that which he did not know
٦-كَلَّآ إِنَّ ٱلإِنْسَٰنَ	*'Kallā 'inna-(a)l-'insāna*	Nay! indeed Man, human kind
لَيَطْغَىٰٓ	*la-yatghā*	surely,transgresses all bounds,
٧- أَن رَّءَاهُ	*'An-ra'ā-hu*	In that he looks (upon himself)
ٱسْتَغْنَىٰٓ	*'istaghnā*	as independent, as self-sufficient
٨-إِنَّ إِلَىٰ	*'Inna 'ilā*	Indeed, surely, verily unto, to
رَبِّكَ ٱلرُّجْعَىٰٓ	*Rabbi-ka-(a)r-ruj'ā*	your Lord is the return
٩-أَرَءَيْتَ	*'A-ra'aita*	Have you seen
ٱلَّذِى يَنْهَىٰ	*'alladhī yanhā*	He who forbids

١٠-عَبْداً	*'Abdan*	A Servant, a slave
إِذَا صَلَّىٰ	*'idhā ṣallā*	when he prays
١١-أَرَءَيْتَ	*'Ara'aita*	Have you seen
إِنْ كَانَ	*'in kāna*	if he was (he is)
عَلَى ٱلْهُدَىٰ	*'ala-(a)l-hudā*	on (the road) of Guidance
١٢-أَوْ أَمَرَ	*'Aw 'amara*	Or enjoins
بِٱلتَّقْوَىٰ	*bi-(a)t-taqwa*	Piety, Righteousness
١٣-أَرَءَيْتَ	*'A-ra'aita*	Have you seen
إِنْ كَذَّبَ	*'in kadhdhaba*	if he denies (the Truth)
وَتَوَلَّىٰ	*wa-tawallā*	and turns away
١٤-أَلَمْ يَعْلَمْ	*'Alam ya'lam*	Does not he know
بِأَنَّ ٱللَّهَ يَرَىٰ	*bi-'anna-(A)llāha yarā*	that Allah sees
١٥-كَلَّا	*Kallā*	Nay, (let him beware)
لَئِنْ لَّمْ يَنْتَهِ	*la'in lam yantahi*	if he does not desist
لَنَسْفَعًا	*la-nasfa'an*	We will drag him
بِٱلنَّاصِيَةِ	*bi-(a)n-nāṣiyah(ti)*	by the forelock
١٦-نَاصِيَةٍ كَاذِبَةٍ	*Nāṣiyatin kādhibatin*	The forelock, a lying
خَاطِئَةٍ	*khāṭi'ah(tin)*	a sinful
١٧-فَلْيَدْعُ نَادِيَهُ	*Fal-yad'u nādiya-hū*	Then let him call (for help)
١٨-سَنَدْعُ ٱلزَّبَانِيَةَ	*Sa-nad'u-(a)z-zabāniyah(ta)*	We will call on the Angels of punishment
١٩-كَلَّا لَا تُطِعْهُ	*Kalla la tuṭi'-hu*	Nay, do not obey him
وَٱسْجُدْ وَٱقْتَرِبْ	*wa-(a)sjud wa-(a)qtarib*	and prostrate, and draw near

Lesson 21 سُوْرَةُ التِّيْنِ

AT-TĪN, 95:1-8

THE FIG / THE FIG

Revealed in Makkah

INTRODUCTION:

This is an early Makkan *Sūrah*. Allāh (SWT) swears by four sacred symbols, to emphasize the importance of His best creation, human being, and its degradation to the lowest status by refusing to heed His Commandments.

TRANSLITERATION:	**ARABIC TEXT:**
Bismillāhi-(a)r-Raḥmāni-(a)r-Raḥīm(i)	بِسْمِ اللّٰهِ الرَّحْمٰنِ الرَّحِيْمِ
1. *Wa-(a)t-tīni wa-(a)z-zaitūn(i)*	وَالتِّيْنِ وَالزَّيْتُوْنِ ۝
2. *Wa ṭūri sīnīn(a)*	وَطُوْرِ سِيْنِيْنَ ۝
3. *Wa hā<u>dh</u>a-(a)l-baladi-(a)l-'amīn(i)*	وَهٰذَا الْبَلَدِ الْاَمِيْنِ ۝
4. *Laqad <u>kh</u>alaqna-(a)l-'insāna fī 'aḥsani taqwīm(in)*	لَقَدْ خَلَقْنَا الْاِنْسَانَ فِيْٓ اَحْسَنِ تَقْوِيْمٍ ۝
5. *<u>Th</u>umma radadnā-hu 'asfala sāfilīn(a)*	ثُمَّ رَدَدْنٰهُ اَسْفَلَ سٰفِلِيْنَ ۝
6. *'Illa-(a)l-la<u>dh</u>īna 'āmanū*	اِلَّا الَّذِيْنَ اٰمَنُوْا
wa 'amilu-(a)ṣ-ṣāliḥāti fa-la-hum	وَعَمِلُوا الصّٰلِحٰتِ فَلَهُمْ
'ajrun <u>gh</u>airu mamnūn(in)	اَجْرٌ غَيْرُ مَمْنُوْنٍ ۝
7. *Fa-mā yuka<u>dh</u>-<u>dh</u>ibu-ka ba'du bi-(a)d-dīn(i)*	فَمَا يُكَذِّبُكَ بَعْدُ بِالدِّيْنِ ۝
8. *'Alais-Allāhu bi-'aḥkami-(a)l-ḥākimīn(a)*	اَلَيْسَ اللّٰهُ بِاَحْكَمِ الْحٰكِمِيْنَ ۝

TRANSLATIONS:

In the name of Allāh, Most Gracious, Most Merciful.

1. By the Fig and the Olive,
2. And the Mount of Sinai,
3. And this City of security,
4. We have indeed created man in the best of molds,
5. Then do We abase him (to be) the lowest of the low,
6. Except such as believe and do righteous deeds: for they shall have a reward unfailing
7. Then what can, after this, contradict you, as to the Judgment (to come)?
8. Is not Allāh the wisest of judges?

In the name of Allāh, the Beneficent, the Merciful.

1. By the fig and the olive,
2. By Mount Sinai,
3. And by this land made safe;
4. Surely We created man of the best stature
5. Then We reduced him to the lowest of the low,
6. Save those who believe and do good works, and theirs is a reward unfailing.
7. So who henceforth will give the lie to you about the Judgment?
8. Is not Allāh the most conclusive of all judges?

EXPLANATION:

95.1. The symbol of the two fruits, the fig and the olive, has two meanings. It makes obvious reference to the exceptional qualities associated with the fruit, but it also refers to the two lands, Syria and Palestine, with which the two fruits are associated. Syria and Palestine are also lands associated with Allāh's Revelation and Prophecy. We shall see the significance of this oath in the following notes.

95:2-3. The *Ṭūr* at Sinai refers to the mountain on which the *Tawrāh* (Torah) was revealed to Mūsā (A), and the City of Security refers to Makkah, where the Ka'bah is located. Makkah was known to be a sacred and secure place for all people, even before the advent of Islam. It became the center of Allāh's Final Revelation, the Qur'ān.

95:4. Allāh (SWT) swears by four of the most important places in the history of Revelation to emphasize the importance of the statement: "We have created man in the best mold." Human beings are the best of all creations in their physical appearance as well as in the endowment of their mental and spiritual qualities.

Allāh (SWT), in His kindness, has blessed human beings with His Revelations. Allāh's Revelations were sent to all human beings to elevate them to their highest spiritual potentials. If they follow the Divine Law, they will live up to their best mold.

95:5. If they reject the Law to follow their own whims and desires, they will be reduced to the lowest of the low. Humans have the potential to rise to great heights. Allāh (SWT) has chosen man as His *Khalīfah* (Vice-gerent) on Earth; and, because of his capabilities, has raised him over the rank of Angels.

95:6. One exception to this rule is that the group of people who believe and do righteous deeds, for them, there is a great reward both in this world and in the Hereafter.

95:7-8. Since human beings have been granted freedom to choose between remaining true to their best mold or falling down to the lowest of the low, it is logical to judge between these two groups. Allāh (SWT), the Creator and the Wisest of all Judges, will Judge in this world and, more importantly, will Judge in the Hereafter. He will reward those who followed the Revelation and punish those who, in spite of His Message, did not heed the call of His Prophets.

WE HAVE LEARNED:

* Allāh (SWT) has created human beings with the potential to rise to their best nature or to fall to their lowest level.
* He has sent Revelations throughout history to all human beings for their guidance.
* With the Revelation of the Qur'ān, human beings are offered an opportunity to realize their best potential and to become worthy of Allāh's favors.

VOCABULARY

٩٥-سُورَةُ ٱلتِّين

١-وَٱلتِّين	*Wa-(a)t-tīni*	By the fig
وَٱلزَّيْتُون	*wa-(a)z-zaitūni*	and the olive
٢-وَطُورِ سِينِينَ	*Wa-ṭūri sīnīn(a)*	And the Mount of Sinai
٣-وَهَٰذَا	*Wa-hādha*	And this
ٱلبَلَدِ ٱلأَمِين	*'Al-baladi-(a)l-'Amīn(i)*	City (of) Security (Makkah)
٤-لَقَدْ	*Laqad*	Surely, indeed
خَلَقْنَا ٱلإِنسَٰنَ	*khalaq-Na-(a)l-'insāna*	We have created Man
فِيٓ أَحْسَنِ تَقْوِيمٍ	*fī 'aḥsani taqwīm(in)*	in the best (of) molds

٥-ثُمَّ رَدَدْنَٰهُ	*Thumma radadnā-hu*	Then, again We reduced him
أَسْفَلَ سَٰفِلِينَ	*'asfala sāfilīn(a)*	the lowest (of) the low
٦-إِلَّا ٱلَّذِينَ	*'Illa-lladhīna*	Except those who
ءَامَنُوا	*'āmanū*	believe, believed
وَعَمِلُوا	*wa -'amilū*	and do, and did
الصَّٰلِحَٰتِ	*'aṣ-ṣāliḥāt(i)*	righteous deeds
فَلَهُمْ أَجْرٌ	*fa-la-hum 'ajrun*	for them will be a reward
غَيْرُ مَمْنُونٍ	*ghairu mamnūn(in)*	unfailing
٧-فَمَا	*Fa-mā*	Then what
يُكَذِّبُكَ	*yu-kadhibu-ka*	contradict you
بَعْدُ بِٱلدِّينِ	*ba'du bi-d-Dīni*	after this as to the Judgment
٨-أَلَيْسَ ٱللَّهُ	*'Alaisa-(A)llāhu*	Is not Allah?
بِأَحْكَمِ	*bi-'Aḥkami*	the Wisest (of)
الْحَٰكِمِينَ	*'al-ḥākimīn(a)*	the judges

Lesson 22

سورة الشرح

AL-'INSHIRĀḤ, 94:1-8

THE EXPANSION OF THE BREAST / SOLACE

Revealed in Makkah

INTRODUCTION:

This *Sūrah*, along with the *Sūrah Aḍ-Ḍuḥā* 94, was revealed in the early Makkan period. The purpose of this Revelation was to console Rasūlullāh (S) for the opposition that he was receiving from the *Kuffār* . In the early stages of his *Da'wah* work, he faced bitter oppostion and insults. Allāh (SWT) recounts His Favors to Rasūlullāh (S), and promises that the future will be easier. These verses are a message for Muslims everywhere to have faith in Allāh's Mercy and be assured of His Help.

TRANSLITERATION:	**ARABIC TEXT:**
Bismillāhi-(a)r-Raḥmāni-(a)r-Raḥīm(i)	بِسْمِ اللَّهِ الرَّحْمَٰنِ الرَّحِيمِ
1. *'Alam nashraḥ la-ka ṣadra-k(a)*	-أَلَمْ نَشْرَحْ لَكَ صَدْرَكَ ۝
2. *Wa waḍa'nā 'an-ka wizra-k(a)*	-وَوَضَعْنَا عَنكَ وِزْرَكَ ۝
3. *'Alladhī 'anqaḍa ẓahra-k(a)*	-الَّذِي أَنقَضَ ظَهْرَكَ ۝
4. *Wa rafa'nā la-ka dhikra-k(a)*	-وَرَفَعْنَا لَكَ ذِكْرَكَ ۝
5. *Fa'inna ma'al'usri yusrā(n)*	-فَإِنَّ مَعَ الْعُسْرِ يُسْرًا ۝
6. *'Inna ma'a-(a)l-'usri yusrā(n)*	-إِنَّ مَعَ الْعُسْرِ يُسْرًا ۝
7. *Fa-'idhā faraghta fa-nṣab*	-فَإِذَا فَرَغْتَ فَانصَبْ ۝
8. *Wa 'ilā Rabbi-ka fa-rghab*	-وَإِلَىٰ رَبِّكَ فَارْغَب ۝

TRANSLATIONS:

In the name of Allāh, Most Gracious,
Most Merciful.

1. Have we not expanded (for) you your breast?
2. And removed from you your burden
3. The which did gall your back?
4. And raised high the esteem
(in which) you (are held)?
5. So, truly with every difficulty, there is relief:
6. Truly, with every difficulty there is relief.
7. Therefore, when you are free
(from your immediate task), still labor hard,
8. And to your Lord turn (all) your attention.

In the name of Allāh, the Beneficent,
the Merciful.

1. Have We not caused your bosom to dilate.
2. And eased you of the burden
3. Which weighed down your back;
4. And exalted
your fame?
5. But lo! with hardship goes ease,
6. Lo! with hardship goes ease;
7. So when you are relieved,
still toil
8. And strive to please your Lord.

EXPLANATION:

94:1-4. Allāh (SWT) begins this *Sūrah* by recounting three special blessings given to Rasūlullāh (S). First, his chest had been expanded; second, his burden had been removed; and third, his name is exalted to this day.

The expanding of Rasūlullāh's chest has two meanings: his chest was cleansed and purified to receive the Divine Revelation, and during childhood, his breast had been opened by the Angels, and his heart literally cleaned. The Revelation relieved his burden: it came with a clear guide to improve the conditions of his people, and of humanity as a whole.

The opposition of the *kuffār* was not able to stop the success of Islam. The promise of great love and respect that Rasūlullāh (S) would gain among his followers is one that had not only been fulfilled during his life-time; but is continuing to be fulfilled to this day, as the message of Islam spreads, and love for Rasūlullāh (S) continues to grow among his followers.

94:5-6. At a time of great opposition and great difficulties, Allāh (SWT) very clearly promises a time of ease, which will soon be at hand. This promise was in reference to Rasūlullāh's personal circumstances, as well as to his task of spreading the message of Islam.

94:7-8. The work of prophethood is never-ending. Thus, when Rasūlullāh (S) was free from his immediate tasks, he continued his efforts for the cause of Islam. These efforts were of two kinds: continuity in the work of *Da'wah*, and constancy in the worship of Allāh (SWT).

Allāh (SWT) is the Ultimate Source of success or failure. All actions of the believers must be directed to please Him alone. Rasūlullāh (S) has not only set the best example for his *'Ummah* by continuously working for the cause of Islam, but he also constantly spent his time in the worship of Allāh (SWT).

WE HAVE LEARNED:

* For Rasūlullāh (S), and for all those who follow him, Allāh's Favors will be unending.
* A Believer should never be discouraged by his immediate difficulties.
* During hardship, a Believer must not despair, but rather should turn to Allāh (SWT) with sincere prayers, seeking His Help and Mercy.

VOCABULARY

٩٤-سُورَةُ ٱلشَّرْحِ

١-أَلَمْ نَشْرَحْ	*'A-lam nashraḥ*	Have not We caused to expand
لَكَ صَدْرَكَ	*la-ka ṣadra-ka*	for you your breast
٢-وَوَضَعْنَا	*Wa-waḍa'na*	We eased, We removed
عَنْكَ	*'an-ka*	from you
وِزْرَكَ	*wizra-ka*	your burden
٣-ٱلَّذِى	*'Alladhi*	That which
أَنْقَضَ	*'anqaḍa*	weighed down
ظَهْرَكَ	*ẓahra-ka*	your back
٤-وَرَفَعْنَا	*Wa-rafa'na*	And We exalted, and We raised high
لَكَ ذِكْرَكَ	*la-ka dhikra-ka*	for you, your fame

٥-فَإِنَّ	*Fa-'inna*	So! but lo! indeed, surely
مَعَ ٱلْعُسْرِ	*ma'a-(a)l-'usri*	with hardship
يُسْراً	*yusran*	ease, relief
٦-إِنَّ مَعَ	*'Inna ma'a*	Truly, indeed with
اَلْعُسْرِ	*'al-'usri*	the hardship
يُسْراً	*yusrā(n)*	ease, relief
٧-فَإِذَا	*Fa-'idhā*	So when,
فَرَغْتَ	*faraghta*	you are free,
فَٱنصَبْ	*fa-(a)nṣab*	still toil, still work hard
٨-وَإِلَىٰ	*Wa-'ilā*	And to
رَبِّكَ	*Rabbi-ka*	your Lord
فَٱرْغَبْ	*fa-(a)rghab*	strive to please, turn your attention

H-W 1-8

Lesson 23

سُورَةُ الضُّحَىٰ

'AḌ-ḌUḤĀ, 93:1-11

THE GLORIOUS MORNING LIGHT / THE MORNING HOURS

Revealed in Makkah

INTRODUCTION:

This *Sūrah* belongs to the early Makkan period. It makes reference to a gap in Revelation that caused Rasūlullāh (S) to become discouraged. At this time, his sole desire had been to receive and spread the Message, and he was worried that, for some reason, the discontinuation in Revelation was a sign of Allāh's displeasure with him. This *Sūrah* consoles Rasūlullāh (S), and reminds him of the great favors that Allāh (SWT) had bestowed upon him. The *Sūrah* also commands him to show gratitude for Allāh's Favors by acting righteously toward others.

TRANSLITERATION:	**ARABIC TEXT:**
Bismillāhi-(a)r-Raḥmāni-r-Raḥīm(i)	بِسْمِ اللَّهِ الرَّحْمَٰنِ الرَّحِيمِ
1. *Wa-(a)ḍ-ḍuḥā*	وَالضُّحَىٰ ۝ -1
2. *Wa-(a)l-laili 'idhā sajā*	وَاللَّيْلِ إِذَا سَجَىٰ ۝ -2
3. *Mā wadda'a-ka Rabbu-ka wa mā qalā*	مَا وَدَّعَكَ رَبُّكَ وَمَا قَلَىٰ ۝ -3
4. *Wa la-l 'ākhiratu khairun la-ka mina-(a)l-'ūlā*	وَلَلْآخِرَةُ خَيْرٌ لَّكَ مِنَ الْأُولَىٰ ۝ -4
5. *Wa la-sawfa yu'ṭī-ka Rabbu-ka fa-tarḍā*	وَلَسَوْفَ يُعْطِيكَ رَبُّكَ فَتَرْضَىٰ ۝ -5
6. *'A-lam yajid-ka yatīman fa'āwā*	أَلَمْ يَجِدْكَ يَتِيمًا فَآوَىٰ ۝ -6
7. *Wa wajada-ka ḍāllan fa-hadā*	وَوَجَدَكَ ضَالًّا فَهَدَىٰ ۝ -7
8. *Wa wajada-ka 'ā'ilan fa-'aghnā*	وَوَجَدَكَ عَائِلًا فَأَغْنَىٰ ۝ -8
9. *Fa'amma-(a)l-yatīma fa-lā taqhar*	فَأَمَّا الْيَتِيمَ فَلَا تَقْهَرْ ۝ -9

10. *Wa 'amma-(a)s-sā'ila fa-lā tanhar* وَأَمَّا السَّائِلَ فَلَا تَنْهَرْ ۝

11. *Wa 'ammā bini`mati Rabbi-ka fa-ḥaddi<u>th</u>* وَأَمَّا بِنِعْمَةِ رَبِّكَ فَحَدِّثْ ۝

<u>TRANSLATIONS</u>:

In the name of Allāh, Most Gracious, Most Merciful.

1. By the Glorious Morning Light,
2. And by the Night when it is still,
3. Your Guardian-Lord has not forsaken you, nor is He displeased.
4. And truly the Hereafter will be better for you than the present.
5. And soon will your Guardian-Lord give you (that with which) you shall be well pleased.
6. Did He not find you an orphan and give you shelter (and care)?
7. And He found you wandering, and He gave you guidance.
8. And He found you in need, and made you independent.
9. Thus, treat not the orphan with harshness
10. Nor repulse the petitioner (unheard);
11. But the Bounty of your Lord rehearse and proclaim.

In the name of Allāh, the Beneficent, the Merciful.

1. By the morning hours
2. And by the night when it is still,
3. Your Lord has not forsaken you nor does He hate you ,
4. And verily the later portion will be better for you than the former
5. And verily your Lord will give unto you so that you will be content.
6. Did He not find you an orphan and protect (you) ?
7. Did He not find you wandering and direct (you)?
8. Did He not find you destitute and enrich (you)?
9. Therefore the orphan oppress not,
10. Therefore the beggar drive not away,
11. Therefore of bounty of your Lord be your discourse.

<u>EXPLANATION</u>:

93:1-2. In these verses, Allāh (SWT) swears by the bright light of day and by the dark stillness of the night. Both these conditions of day and night are symbols of Allāh's Infinite Power. The brightness of the day is as important for working, as the stillness of the night is for resting.

93:3. The Revelation to Rasūlullāh (S) was discontinued for sometime. In various traditions, this period is estimated to have lasted between twelve and forty days. For Rasūlullāh (S), this time was very difficult. He began to imagine that he might have committed a mistake and therefore, in some way, deserve Allāh's displeasure. Some of the *Kuffār* began to taunt him about this.

Allāh (SWT) then informed Rasūlullāh (S) that He had not abandoned him, nor was He angry with him. As the day and night are Signs of Allāh (SWT), so was the Revelation's continuity (representing light of the day) or discontinuity (representing the darkness of the night).

93:4-5. Although Rasūlullāh (S) experienced great opposition from the *Kuffār*, he was promised a better future for himself and for his message. This promise holds true in this world as well as in the Hereafter. Allāh (SWT) promised that His Blessings would be so great that Rasūlullāh (S) would be pleased and satisfied.

93:6-8. Allāh (SWT) reminds Rasūlullāh (S) of the great favors granted to him in the past. He had been left an orphan and Allāh (SWT) had protected him. He had been wandering, in search of the truth, and Allāh (SWT) now provided him with Guidance. He had been poor and Allāh (SWT) had made him financially independent.

These reassuring description of Allāh's many blessings prompted Rasūlullāh (S) to reciprocate; by giving thanks to Allāh (SWT) and doing good for those who were disadvantaged.

93:9-10. For His kindness, Allāh (SWT) asked of Rasūlullāh (S) two specific, and one general, things. He was commanded to show kindness to orphans, as Allāh (SWT) had been kind to him. He was commanded to be kind and polite to a *sā'il*, when he asked for help. Finally, he was commanded to proclaim the Greatness of Allāh (SWT).

WHO IS A SĀ'IL?

The Arabic term *sā'il* means "one who seeks help" or "one who asks a question." A person needing help may be a poor or a needy, requesting assistance. This person must be helped, or if we can't help then politely refused. A person with a question must be listened to and answered in a decent manner, or if his queston is to be declined, it must be done so decently. The position we must adopt, therefore, is one of decency and politeness towards one who comes to us for any kind of help.

93:11. Rasūlullāh (S) is enjoined to proclaim the Blessings of Allāh (SWT). Some of those blessings are mentioned in this *Sūrah*, but they are infinite, and cannot be described by mere words. There are various ways in which we proclaim and describe these Blessings. First, we may acknowledge them in our hearts; second, we may recite them with our tongues; and most importantly, we acknowledge them by trying to do similar favors unto others.

WHAT WE HAVE LEARNED:

* At times, we are in diffculties Allāh's Favors are with us.
* The Favors and Mercies of Allāh (SWT) are limitless and they are constantly with us.
* We must show our thankfulness to Him by showing consideration to others.

VOCABULARY

٩٣- سورة ٱلضُّحَىٰ

١-وَٱلضُّحَىٰ	*Wa-(a)ḍ-ḍuḥā*	By the morning
٢-وَٱلَّيْلِ	*Wa-(a)l-laili*	And by the night
إِذَا سَجَىٰ	*'idhā sajā*	when it covers
٣-مَا وَدَّعَكَ	*Mā wadda'a-ka*	Has not forsaken you
رَبُّكَ	*Rabbu-ka*	your Lord
وَمَا قَلَىٰ	*wa mā-qalā*	and nor He is displeased
٤-وَلَلْآخِرَةُ	*Wa-lal-'ākhiratu*	And surely, the Hereafter
خَيْرٌ لَّكَ	*khairun la-ka*	will be better for you
مِنَ ٱلْأُولَىٰ	*mina-(a)l-'ūlā*	than the present life
٥-وَلَسَوْفَ يُعْطِيكَ	*Wa-lasawfa yu'ṭīka*	And (soon) will give you
رَبُّكَ	*Rabbu-ka*	your Lord
فَتَرْضَىٰ	*fa-tarḍā*	So that you will be pleased, content
٦-أَلَمْ يَجِدْكَ	*'Alam yajid-ka*	Did not He find you
يَتِيمًا	*yatīm(an)*	an orphan
فَـَٔاوَىٰ	*fa-'āwā*	and He protected you, so He gave you shelter
٦-وَوَجَدَكَ ضَآلًّا	*Wa-wajada-ka ḍāllan*	And He found you wandering
فَهَدَىٰ	*fa-hadā*	so He guided
٨-وَوَجَدَكَ عَآئِلًا	*Wa-wajada-ka 'ā'ilan*	and He found you in need
فَأَغْنَىٰ	*fa-'aghnā*	so He enriched you, made you independent
٩-فَأَمَّا ٱلْيَتِيمَ	*Fa-'amma-(a)l-yatīma*	Therefore, as for the orphan

فَلاَ تَقْهَرْ	*fa-lā taqhar*	so, do not oppress
١٠-وَأَمَّا ٱلسَّآئِلَ	*Wa-'ammā-s-sā'ila*	as for the one who asks
فَلاَ تَنْهَرْ	*fa-lā tanhar*	so, do not drive away, (repulse)
١١-وَأَمَّا	*Wa-'ammā*	And , as for
بِنِعْمَةِ رَبِّكَ	*bi-ni'mati Rabbi-ka*	the bounty of your Lord
فَحَدِّثْ	*fa-ḥaddi<u>th</u>*	so, rehearse, proclaim

Lesson 24

سُورَةُ اللَّيْلِ

AL-LAIL, 92:1-10

THE NIGHT / THE NIGHT

Revealed in Makkah

INTRODUCTION:

This *Sūrah* is one of the first ten *Suwar* to be revealed in Makkah. It is similar in subject matter to *As<u>h</u>-<u>Sh</u>ams*, (91).

It contrasts two types of people, the charitable and the miserly, and describes each of their characteristics.

TRANSLITERATION:	**ARABIC TEXT:**
Bismillāhi-(a)r-Raḥmāni-(a)r-Raḥīm(i)	بِسْمِ اللَّهِ الرَّحْمَٰنِ الرَّحِيمِ
1. *Wa-(a)l-laili 'i<u>dh</u>ā ya<u>gh</u>s<u>h</u>ā*	وَاللَّيْلِ إِذَا يَغْشَىٰ ۝ -١
2. *Wā-(a)n-nahāri 'i<u>dh</u>ā tajallā*	وَالنَّهَارِ إِذَا تَجَلَّىٰ ۝ -٢
3. *Wa mā <u>kh</u>alaqa-(a)<u>dh</u>-<u>dh</u>akara wa-(a)l-'un<u>th</u>ā*	وَمَا خَلَقَ الذَّكَرَ وَالْأُنثَىٰ ۝ -٣
4. *'Inna sa'ya-kum lā<u>sh</u>attā*	إِنَّ سَعْيَكُمْ لَشَتَّىٰ ۝ -٤
5. *Fā'ammā man 'a'ṭā wa-(a)t-taqā*	فَأَمَّا مَنْ أَعْطَىٰ وَاتَّقَىٰ ۝ -٥
6. *Wa ṣaddaqa bi-(a)l-ḥusnā*	وَصَدَّقَ بِالْحُسْنَىٰ ۝ -٦
7. *Fa-sa-nuyassiru-hū li-(a)l-yusrā*	فَسَنُيَسِّرُهُ لِلْيُسْرَىٰ ۝ -٧
8. *Wa 'ammā man ba<u>kh</u>ila wā-(i)sta<u>gh</u>nā*	وَأَمَّا مَن بَخِلَ وَاسْتَغْنَىٰ ۝ -٨
9. *Wa ka<u>dhdh</u>aba bi-(a)l-ḥusnā*	وَكَذَّبَ بِالْحُسْنَىٰ ۝ -٩
10. *Fa-sa-nuyassiru-hū li-(a)l-'usrā*	فَسَنُيَسِّرُهُ لِلْعُسْرَىٰ ۝ -١٠

TRANSLATIONS:

In the name of Allāh, Most Gracious, Most Merciful.	In the name of Allāh, the Beneficent, the Merciful.
1. By the Night as it conceals (the light);	1. By the night enshrouding
2. By the Day as it appears in glory;	2. And the day resplendent
3. By (the mystery of) the creation of male and female;	3. And Him who has created male and female,
4. Truly, (the ends) you strive for are diverse	4. Lo! your effort is dispersed (toward diverse ends).
5. So he who gives (in charity) and fears (Allāh),	5. As for him who gives and is dutiful (toward Allāh)
6. And (in all sincerity) testifies to the Best,	6. And believes in goodness;
7. We will indeed make smooth for him the path to Bliss.	7. Surely We will ease his way unto the state of ease.
8. But he who is a greedy miser and thinks himself self-sufficient,	8. But as for him who hoards and deems himself independent,
9. And gives the lie to the Best,	9. And disbelieves in goodness;
10. We will indeed make smooth for him the Path to Misery;	10. Surely We will ease his way into adversity.

EXPLANATION:

92:1-2. In these *'Āyāt*, night and day are contrasted in a similar fashion, as in the previous *Sūrah*: night and day have been created to fulfill a specific purpose in Allāh's Plan.

92:3. Allāh (SWT) has created another contrast of male and female. They both originate from a single source, yet they are very different from each other, and in the Divine Scheme, they complement one another. The harmony of their co-existence serves to fulfill the Divine Purpose of Creation.

92:4. All human beings must strive to achieve their goals, but their struggles may be of different natures. Some follow the path of righteousness while others follow that of falsehood.

92:5-7. There are those who give generously in charity, fear Allāh (SWT) and support and testify to the Truth. Allāh (SWT) will ease their way in this world and in the Hereafter. The ease of this world is world is considered to be peace of mind and consolation of the soul. This can never be measured by any worldly standards of wealth or material increments.

92:8-10. Then there are those who are miserly and do not give of their wealth; they are proud and think themselves independent of Allāh's Will. They oppose and refute the Truth, and Allāh (SWT) will make their path difficult in this world and in the Hereafter. In this world, such people, driven by greed, find no peace of mind or consolation of the soul. Their worldly goods are not sufficient to offer them real peace and comfort.

WE HAVE LEARNED:

* All human beings strive to achieve certain goals in life.
* Some are generous and righteous, Allāh (SWT) makes things easy for them.
* Some are miser and proud, Allāh (SWT) makes things difficult for them.

VOCABULARY

٩٢-سُورَةُ ٱللَّيْل

١-وَٱلَّيل	*Wa-(a)l-laili*	By the night
إِذَا يَغْشَىٰ	*'idhā yaghshā*	as it enshrouds, when it conceals
٢-وَٱلنَّهارِ	*Wa-(a)n-nahāri*	By the day
إِذَا تَجَلَّىٰ	*'idhā tajallā*	when it is resplendent,
٣-وَمَا خَلَقَ	*Wa-mā khalaqa*	By HimWho created
الذَكَرَ	*adh-dhakara*	the male
وَٱلأُنثَىٰ	*wa-(a)l-'unthā*	and the female
٤-إِنَّ سَعْيَكُمْ	*'Inna sa'ya-kum*	Truly your effort
لَشَتَّىٰ	*la-shattā*	is various, diverse, dispersed
٥-فَأَمَّا مَنْ	*Fa-'ammā man*	As for him who
أَعْطَىٰ	*'a'ṭā*	gives (charity)
وَٱتَّقَىٰ	*wa-(a)t-taqā*	and fears , is righteous

٦-وَصَدَّقَ	*Wa-ṣaddaqa*	And believes , and testifies
بِٱلْحُسْنَىٰ	*bi-(a)l-ḥusnā*	in goodness , to the best
٧-فَسَنُيَسِّرُهُۥ	*Fa-sanuyassiru-hū*	Indeed! We shall make smooth his way
لِلْيُسْرَىٰ	*li-(a)l-yusrā*	to the state of ease
٨-وَأَمَّا مَنْ	*Wa-'ammā man*	And he who
بَخِلَ	*bakhila*	is a miser
وَٱسْتَغْنَىٰ	*wa-(i)staghnā*	and thinks himself self-sufficient,
٩-وَكَذَّبَ	*Wa-kadhdhaba*	And gives lie, refutes
بِٱلْحُسْنَىٰ	*bi-(a)l-ḥusnā*	to the best, to goodness
١٠-فَسَنُيَسِّرُهُۥ	*Fa-sa-nuyassiru-hū*	Indeed ! We shall make smooth for him
لِلْعُسْرَىٰ	*li-(a)l-'usrā*	The path to misery, way to adversity

Lesson 25

AL-LAIL 92:11-21

THE NIGHT / THE NIGHT

Revealed in Makkah

TRANSLITERATION:	**ARABIC TEXT:**
11. Wa mā yughnī `an-hū mālu-hū 'idhā taraddā	-وَمَا يُغْنِىْ عَنْهُ مَالُهٗٓ اِذَا تَرَدّٰى ○
12. 'Inna `alainā la-(a)l-hudā	-اِنَّ عَلَيْنَا لَلْهُدٰى ○
13. Wa 'inna lanā la-(a)l-'ākhirata wa-(a)l-'ūlā	-وَاِنَّ لَنَا لَلْاٰخِرَةَ وَالْاُوْلٰى ○
14. Fa-'andhartu-kum nāran talaẓẓā	-فَاَنْذَرْتُكُمْ نَارًا تَلَظّٰى ○
15. Lā yaṣlā-hā 'illa-(a)l 'ashqa	-لَا يَصْلٰىهَآ اِلَّا الْاَشْقَى ○
16. 'Alladhī kadhdhaba wa tawallā	-الَّذِىْ كَذَّبَ وَتَوَلّٰى ○
17. Wa sa-yujannabu-ha-(a)l-'atqā	-وَسَيُجَنَّبُهَا الْاَتْقَى ○
18. 'Alladhī yu'tī māla-hū yatazakkā	-الَّذِىْ يُؤْتِىْ مَالَهٗ يَتَزَكّٰى ○
19. Wa mā li-'aḥadin `inda-hū min ni`matin tujzā	-وَمَا لِاَحَدٍ عِنْدَهٗ مِنْ نِّعْمَةٍ تُجْزٰٓى ○
20. 'Illa-(i)btighā'a wajhi Rabbi-hi-(a)l-'A`lā	-اِلَّا ابْتِغَآءَ وَجْهِ رَبِّهِ الْاَعْلٰى ○
21. Wa la-sawfa yarḍā	-وَلَسَوْفَ يَرْضٰى ○

TRANSLATIONS:

11. Nor will his wealth profit him when he falls headlong (into the Pit)	11. His riches will not save him when he perishes.
12. Truly We take upon Ourselves to guide,	12. Lo! Ours it is (to give) the guidance
13. And truly unto Us (belong) the End and the Beginning.	13. And lo! unto Us belong the latter portion and the former.

14. Therefore do I warn you of
a Fire Blazing fiercely;
15. None shall reach it but
those most unfortunate ones
16. Who give the lie to Truth
and turn their backs.
17. But those most devoted to Allāh
shall be removed far from it,
18. Those who spend their wealth
for increase in self-purification,
19. And have in their minds no favor
from anyone for which a reward is
expected in return,
20. But only the desire to seek for
the Countenance of their Lord Most High;
21. And soon will they attain
(complete) satisfaction.

14. Therefore have I warned you of
the flaming Fire,
15. Which only the most wretched
must endure,
16. He who denies
and turns away.
17. Far removed from it
will be the righteous
18. Who gives his wealth that he may
grow (in goodness),
19. And none has
with him any
favour for reward,
20. Except as seeking (to fulfil)
the purpose of his Lord Most High.
21. He verily will
be content.

EXPLANATION:

92:11-13. Everything belongs to Allāh (SWT). He is the Master of the Beginning and the End and Guidance comes from Him alone. Worldly goods and position may be temporarily beneficial, but they cannot save a disobedient soul in the Hereafter.

92:14-16. Allāh (SWT) warns of the fierce fire of Hell that awaits those unfortunate people who deny the Truth, even after it has been presented to them and those people who had turned their backs on Rașūlullāh (S) when he invited them to Islam.

92:17:21. The God-fearing person is sharply contrasted to the unfortunate miser. He generously gives his money in the Path of Allāh (SWT), in order to purify it. He seeks no reward for his good deeds because everything is done to please Allāh (SWT) alone. Such a person shall experience complete peace, satisfaction and pleasure from his works and actions.

For every individual, peace and satisfaction may mean different things. However, in this case, these terms do not refer to an abundance of worldly good. Rather, they are taken to mean health, a good family life,

one is at peace with himself and his Lord. The rewards of the Hereafter are permanent and are in addition to what we gain in this life.

WE HAVE LEARNED:

* Human beings, though created from a single source, are divided into two groups: the righteous and the greedy ones.
* Allāh (SWT) is our Creator and to Him is our return.
* Every good deed must be done to please Allāh (SWT) alone.

VOCABULARY II

٩٢-سُورَةُ ٱللَّيْل

١١-وَمَايُغْنِى	*Wa-ma yughnī*	And will not profit ,
عَنْهُ مَالُهُ	*'an-hu mālu-hū*	to him his wealth
إِذَا تَرَدَّىٰ	*'idhā taraddā*	when he perishes, when he falls headlong
١٢-إِنَّ عَلَيْنَا	*'Inna 'alai-Na*	Truly! upon Ourselves, indeed Ours it is
لَلْهُدَىٰ	*lal-hudā*	to guide
١٣-وَإِنَّ لَنَا	*Wa-'inna la-Nā*	And truly unto Us
لَلأَخِرَةَ	*la-l-'ākhirata*	belongs the end, the later part
وَٱلأُولَىٰ	*wa-l-'ūlā*	and the beginning, the former part
١٤-فَأَنْذَرْتُكُمْ	*Fa-'andhartu-kum*	Therefore, I warn you
نَاراً تَلَظَّىٰ	*nāran talazza*	fire blazing fiercely, flaming fire
لاَ يَصْلَٰهَا	*lā yaslā-hā*	none shall reach it, none will endure
إِلاَّ ٱلأَشْقَىٰ	*'illa-(a)l-'ashqā*	but those most unfortunate
١٦-الَّذِى كَذَّبَ	*'Alladhī kadhdhaba*	He who denies (theTruth)
وَتَوَلَّىٰ	*wa-tawallā*	and turns away, and turns his back

١٧-وَسَيُجَنَّبُهَا	*Wa-sa-yujannabu-hā*	And shall be far removed from it
الأَتْقَىٰ	*'al-'atqā*	the most righteous, the most devoted,
١٨-الَّذِى يُؤْتِى	*'Alladhī yu'tī*	He who gives, spends
مَالَهُ	*māla-hū*	his wealth
يَتَزَكَّىٰ	*yatazakkā*	for increase in self-purification, to grow in goodness
١٩-وَمَا لِأَحَدٍ	*Wa-mā li-'aḥadin*	And not from anyone
عِنْدَهُ	*'inda-hū*	from Him, with Him
مِنْ نِعْمَةٍ	*min ni'matin*	of a reward, of a favor
تُجْزَىٰ	*tujzā*	to be expected, to be bestowed
٢٠-إِلاَّ ٱبْتِغَاءَ	*'Illa-(i)btighā'a*	But only the desire, (of)
وَجْهِ	*wajhi*	the pleasure (of)
رَبِّهِ الأَعْلَىٰ	*Rabbi-hi-(a)l-'A'lā*	His Lord the Most High
٢١-وَلَسَوْفَ يَرْضَىٰ	*Wa-la-sawfa yarḍā*	And he shall be satisfied

Lesson 26 سورة الشمس

ASH-SHAMS, 91:1-15

THE SUN / THE SUN

Revealed in Makkah

INTRODUCTION:

This *Sūrah* belongs to the early Makkan period, during the time when the Muslims faced great opposition from the *Kuffār*. The central subject of the *Sūrah* is the creation of the human soul, and its inherent ability to choose between good and evil. This theme is explained further, with the help of the story of Prophet Ṣāliḥ (A) and his camel.

TRANSLITERATION:	**ARABIC TEXT**:
Bismillāhi-(a)r-Raḥmāni-(a)r-Raḥīm(i)	بِسْمِ اللّٰهِ الرَّحْمٰنِ الرَّحِيْمِ
1. *Wa-shshamsi wa ḍuḥā-hā*	وَالشَّمْسِ وَضُحٰهَا ۝
2. *Wa-(a)l-qamari 'idhā talā-hā*	وَالْقَمَرِ إِذَا تَلٰهَا ۝
3. *Wa-(a)n-nahāri 'idhā jallā-hā*	وَالنَّهَارِ إِذَا جَلّٰهَا ۝
4. *Wa-(a)l-laili 'idhā yaghshā-hā*	وَالَّيْلِ إِذَا يَغْشٰهَا ۝
5. *Wa-(a)s-samā'i wa mā banā-hā*	وَالسَّمَآءِ وَمَا بَنٰهَا ۝
6. *Wa-(a)l 'arḍi wa mā ṭaḥā-hā*	وَالْأَرْضِ وَمَا طَحٰهَا ۝
7. *Wa nafsin wa mā sawwā-hā*	وَنَفْسٍ وَّمَا سَوّٰهَا ۝
8. *Fa-'alhama-hā fujūra-hā wa-taqwā-hā*	فَأَلْهَمَهَا فُجُوْرَهَا وَتَقْوٰهَا ۝
9. *Qad 'aflaḥa man zakkā-hā*	قَدْ أَفْلَحَ مَنْ زَكّٰهَا ۝
10. *Wa qad khāba man dassā-hā*	وَقَدْ خَابَ مَنْ دَسّٰهَا ۝

11. Kadhdhabat thamūdu bi-ṭaghwā-hā

-كَذَّبَتْ ثَمُودُ بِطَغْوٰهَآ ۝

12. 'Idhin ba`atha 'ashqā-hā

-اِذِ انْبَعَثَ اَشْقٰهَا ۝

13. Fa-qāla la-hum Rasūlullāhi nāqata-(A)llāhi wa suqyā-hā

-فَقَالَ لَهُمْ رَسُوْلُ اللّٰهِ نَاقَةَ اللّٰهِ وَ سُقْيٰهَا ۝

14. Fakadhdhabū-hu fa-`aqarū-hā fa-damdama `alai-him

Rabbu-hum bi-dhanbi-him fasawwā-hā

-فَكَذَّبُوْهُ فَعَقَرُوْهَا ۥ فَدَمْدَمَ عَلَيْهِمْ

رَبُّهُمْ بِذَنْۢبِهِمْ فَسَوّٰىهَا ۝

15. Wa lā yakhāfu `uqbā-hā

-وَلَا يَخَافُ عُقْبٰهَا ۝

TRANSLATIONS:

In the name of Allāh, Most Gracious,
Most Merciful.

1. By the Sun and his (glorious) splendour;
2. By the Moon as it follows (the Sun);
3. By the Day as it shows up (the Sun's) glory;
4. By the Night as it conceals it;
5. By the Firmament and its (wonderful) structure;
6. By the Earth and its (wide) expanse;
7. By the Soul, and the proportion and 7. order given to it;
8. And its enlightenment as to its wrong and its right;
9. Truly he succeeds that purifies it,
10. And he fails that corrupts it!
11. The Thamūd (people) rejected (their prophet) through their inordinate wrongdoing.
12. Behold, the most wicked man

In the name of Allāh, the Beneficent,
the Merciful.

1. By the sun and his brightness,
2. And the moon when she followes him.
3. And the day when it reveals him,
4. And the night when it enshrouds him,
5. And the heaven and Him Who (wonderfully) built it,
6. And the earth and Him Who spread it,
   And a soul and
   Him Who perfected it
8. And inspired it (with conscience of) what is wrong for it and (what is) right for it.
9. He is indeed successful who causes it to grow,
10. And he is indeed a failure who stunts it.
11. (The tribe of) Thamūd denied (the Truth) in their rebellious pride.
12. When the basest

13. But the Messenger of Allāh said to them: "It is a She-camel of Allāh! and (bar her not from) having her drink!"	13. And the messenger of Allāh said: It is the She-camel of Allāh, so let her drink!
14. Then they rejected him (as a false prophet), and they hamstrung her. So their Lord, on account of their crime, obliterated their traces and made them equal (in destruction, high and low)	14. But they denied him, and they hamstrung her, so Allāh doomed them for their sin and razed (their dwellings).
15. And for Him is no fear of its consequences.	15. He dreadeth not the sequel (of events).

EXPLANATION:

91:1-6. In these verses, Allāh (SWT) swears by six of His creations. These may be placed into three pairs of opposites: the sun and moon, the night and day, and the heaven and earth. These oaths support the statement in verse 7, therefore we must look at these oaths in the light of the message related in this verse.

Besides their inherent usefulness to human beings, these creations symbolize the Power of Allāh (SWT). The conflicting qualities found within the human soul have been created by Allāh (SWT) as a demonstration of His Power. Secondly, these creations are pairs of opposites, and yet, they are a part of the cosmic order that has been established by Allāh (SWT). The opposing forces within us occur naturally, having been created by Allāh (SWT).

91:7. Allāh (SWT) swears by the human soul that He has proportioned and perfected. He has given it a beautiful physical form. We are able to use our bodies to facilitate various functions, as well as to be creative. Allāh has also endowed our souls with intelligence, emotions and judgment.

91:8. Allāh (SWT) has inspired the soul with distinction between right and wrong, and the freedom to choose between the two opposing forces. According to Islam, every human being is born free from sin. Initially, the tendency to follow the Straight Path is dominant within the soul. However, if man does not respond to the call of good conduct and, instead, chooses to behave immorally, the soul loses its sensitivity to goodness and begins to accept evil as a natural way.

91:9-10. Human beings may choose between good and evil. One type of person purifies his soul and conditions it to do good deeds. The other corrupts his soul and stops its healthy growth. Thus, he has failed himself.

He instructed them to allow the she-camel to graze and drink water unhindered. He also warned them of the consequences if they disobeyed his instructions and harmed her.

The people of Thamūd refused to obey Prophet Ṣāliḥ (A). They sent the most wicked from amongst their people to strike the she-camel. As a result of their defiance, they were visited by Allāh's punishment. They were destroyed, and their town was completely levelled to the ground.

91:15. Allāh has the power to create or to destroy. He fears no one.

WE HAVE LEARNED:

* Allāh (SWT) has created in human soul both abilities of choosing good and evil.
* It is our choice which way we choose for ourselves.
* Allāh (SWT) has punished the wicked in the past, and shall punish them in future as well.

VOCABULARY

٩١-سُورَةُ ٱلشَّمْسِ

١-وَٱلشَّمْسِ	*Wa-(a)sh-shamsi*	By the sun
وَضُحَـٰهَا	*wa-ḍuḥā-hā*	And his glorious splendour
٢-وَٱلْقَمَرِ	*Wa-(a)l-qamar(i)*	And the moon
إِذَا تَلَـٰهَا	*'idha talā-hā*	when she follows
٣-وَٱلنَّهَارِ	*Wa-(a)n-nahār(i)*	By the morning
إِذَا جَلَّـٰهَا	*'idhā jallā-hā*	when it shows up glory, when it reveals him
٤-وَٱلَّيْلِ	*Wa-(a)l-lail(i)*	By the night
إِذَا يَغْشَـٰهَا	*'idhā yaghshā-hā*	when enshrouds him
٥-وَٱلسَّمَاءِ	*Wa-(a)s-samā'(i)*	By the sky, Heaven
وَمَا بَنَـٰهَا	*wa-mā banā-hā*	and what built it
٦-وَٱلْأَرْضِ	*Wa-(a)l-'arḍ(i)*	By the Earth
وَمَا طَحَـٰهَا	*wa-ma ṭaḥā-hā*	and what spread it
٧-وَنَفْسٍ	*Wa-nafs(in)*	Amd by the soul
وَمَا سَوَّاهَا	*wa-mā sawwā-hā*	and what perfected it

٨-فَأَلْهَمَهَا	*Fa-'alhama-hā*	So, He inspired it
فُجُورَهَا وَتَقْوٰهَا	*fujūra-hā wa-taqwā-hā*	its wrong and its right
٩- قَدْ أَفْلَحَ	*Qad 'aflaḥa*	Indeed ! he is successful
مَنْ زَكّٰهَا	*man zakkā-hā*	who purifies it, who causes it to grow
١٠-وَقَدْ خَابَ	*Wa-qad khāba*	And he indeed fails
مَنْ دَسّٰهَا	*man dassā-hā*	who corrupts it
١١-كَذَّبَتْ ثَمُودُ	*Kadhdhabat Thamūdu*	rejected Thamud
بِطَغْوٰهَا	*bi-taghwā-hā*	with its rebellious wrong doing
١٢-إِذِ ٱنْبَعَثَ	*'Idhi-n-ba'atha*	When it deputed
أَشْقٰهَا	*'ashqā-hā*	the most wicked of it
١٣-فَقَالَ لَهُمْ	*Fa-qāla la-hum*	So he said to them
رَسُولُ ٱللَّهِ	*Rasulu-(A)llāhi,*	the Messenger of Allah
نَاقَةَ ٱللَّهِ	*nāqata-(A)llāhi*	it is the she -camel of Allah
وَسُقْيٰهَا	*wa-suqyā-hā*	let her drink
١٤-فَكَذَّبُوهُ	*fa-kadhdhabū-hu,*	they denied him
فَعَقَرُوهَا	*fa-'aqarū-hā*	they hamstrung her
فَدَمْدَمَ	*fa-damdama*	crushed
عَلَيْهِمْ	*'alai-him*	upon them
رَبُّهُمْ	*Rabbu-hum*	their Lord
بِذَنْبِهِمْ	*bi-dhanbi-him*	for their sin
فَسَوّٰهَا	*fa-sawwā-hā*	so He obliterated it, razed it (to ground)
١٥-وَلَا يَخَافُ	*Wa-la yakhāfu*	And He does not fear
عُقْبٰهَا	*'uqbā-hā*	its consequence

APPENDIX I:

GLOSSARY

'Abd	Servant (of God)
Abase	To reduce or lower in rank or reputation
Absolute	Free from imperfection
Accusation	A charge of doing something wrong
Ad-dīn	The religion, the Day of Judgment
Advent	Arrival, beginning
Adversity	Problem, misfortune
Al-'Ākhirah	The After Life
Al-Kawthar	The Abundance, A fountain in *Jannah*
Ar-Raḥīm	The Most Merciful
Ar-Raḥmān	The Most Gracious
Arrogance	Pride, showing off
Aṣḥāb al-Fīl	People of Elephant, owners of Elephant
Al-'Aṣr	Time through the ages, the time of evening prayer
Astray	Going out of the right path
Aṣ-Ṣamad	The Eternal
At-Takāthur	The piling up
Aṭ-Ṭūr	Mount Sināi, Mount Ṭūr
'Āyah	Sign, a verse of the Qur'ān, singular of 'Āyah
Backbiting	Attacking the character of a person in his/her absence
Bait-Allāh	House of Allāh, Ka'bah in Makkah
Beneficent	One who does good things
Bereft	Deprived, not having
Blazing	Burning
Bestow	To give
Calamity	Great misfortune
Caravan	Group of travelers
Caretaker	Person who temporarily performs the duties of an office
Charitable	Generous in helping others with money and gifts
Chronicles	Orderly record of events
Clamor	Loud continuous noise
Co-existence	To live side by side in a peaceful manner
Complement	To complete something

Compromise	To mutually reach an agreement
Compulsion	To force someone to do something
Conclusive	Reaching a final decision
Consequence	After effect of something
Consolation	To give comfort to someone who is having problems
Constancy	Faithfulness, to be firm
Consuming	Destroying
Contrast	To compare in order to show the difference
Convulsion	Great disturbance
Cosmic	Universal, the material space outside our earth
Covenant	Agreement
Crackling	Continuous making of a slight sound
Da'wah	Religious propagation
Day of Judgment	The day when all creations would be resurrected and judged
Degradation	Reduction in amount, strength or power
Devoured	To eat up hungrily
Disperse	To scatter in different directions
Distinction	Marked superiority, excellence, special characteristic
Distract	To divert, to disturb
Distress	Great pain
Divine	Anything related to the Supreme Being (God)
Divine Scheme	Plan of God, design of God
Dominance	Rule, Control
Elevate	To raise or lift
Endangerment	To risk, to jeopardize
Endurance	Power to bear pain
Endowment	To provide with permanent funds
Enlightenment	Attainment of intellectual and/or spiritual wisdom
En Masse	All together
Eternal	Forever, Which has neither beginning nor end
Evidence	Proof
Evil-doers	People who do wrong things
Farḍ	Compulsory, obligatory
Farewell pilgrimage	The last pilgrimage of the Prophet (S)
Fiqh	Jurisprudence, Islamic law

Firmament	The vault of heaven
Fount of Abundance	The fount of *Al-Kawthar* in *Jannah*, People will not feel thirsty forever after drinking from this fountain
Gracious	Kind, courteous
Gratitude	The feeling of being thankful
Guardian Lord	Protector, *Rabb*
Guidance	The act of guiding, showing the right path
Hamstrung	To disable by cutting the hamstring at the back of camel, make useless
Harmony	Pleasing arrangement
Heed	To pay attention
Hereafter	The Day of Judgment, *Al-'Ākhirah*
Hoarding	To hide money or food for future profit or gain
Humazah	Scandalmonger, one who makes scandals
Hymn	A song in praise of Allāh (SWT)
Idolatry	Worshipping of idols
Ignorant	Having lack of knowledge
Image	Likeness of a person, animal or thing
'Imām Rāzi	A great Islamic scholar
Immortal	Living forever
Increment	An addition or increase
Indigent	A needy or poor
Infinite	Endless in time and space
Ingrate	Ungrateful person
Inherent	Inborn, innate
Inherit	To acquire or receive
Inordinate	Excessive
Inspire	To encourage, to motivate
Invade	To attack
Intercession	Arbitration or mediation, to plead on behalf of a person
Jahannam	Hell
Jannah	Paradise
Jinn	Creation of God made from fire
Kuffār	Unbelievers, plural of Kāfir

Literal	Exact, precise
Malignant	mean, malevolent
Manifest	Obvious
Martyr	One who dies in the cause of Allāh
Mischief	An injury caused intentionally by another person or agent
Miserly	stingy or thrifty
Mission	A goal, purpose or task
Mold	A matrix, cast or die
Mufassir	One who give explanations
Munāfiqūn	Hypocrites
Mushrikūn	Unbelievers, plural of Mushrik
Muttaqī	Pious person
Naught	Nothing
Oath	A pledge, vow or promise
Obliterate	To destroy or demolish
Oft-returning	Often returning
Ordain	To appoint, select or install
Outstretch	To expand
Pagan	Unbeliever
Panting	To breathe heavily
Pelt	To attack repeatedly
Peninsula	Piece of land mostly surrounded by water
Plunge	To jump into
Polytheists	One who believes in more than one god
Posterity	descendants
Prestige	Reputation
Proclaim	To declare
Prophethood	Life of a person after being assigned as a Prophet
Protector	One who defends or protects
Purified	Made clean
Qanā'ah	Contentment, be satisfied with what Allāh gives
Qāri'ah	Calamity, Calamity of Qiyāmah
Qiyāmah	The Day of Judgment

Quraish An Arab tribe which ruled Makkah

Quraish	An Arab tribe which ruled Makkah
Rabb	Lord, Master, Creator and Sustainer
Raging	Full of anger
Reciprocate	To return, respond or retaliate
Recite	To read
Refuge	To take shelter from danger
Refute	To disapprove, to deny
Render	To make
Repulse	To repel, resist, refuse or throw back
Responsibility	Something for which one is made accountable
Revelation	Allah's disclosure of Himself or His Will to someone, *Waḥī*
Righteous	One who is morally rightful
Rumor	Gossip, a false statement or story
Sacred arts	Arts which are religious or spiritual
Sā'il	One who asks for something
Safeguard	Defence, precaution
Ṣaḥābah	Companions of the Prophet (S), Plural of Ṣaḥābī
Scandal	A shameful action
Scandal monger	One who spreads scandals
Schism	Division
Scouring	Searching
Scripture	Any writing or book of religious nature
Sensitivity	Quality of being easily affected by pain
Shāfā'ah	Intercession, recommendation
Shaiṭān	Satan, Devil
Shayāṭin	plural of satan
Shirk	Unbelief, Association of someone with Allāh
Slander	To circulate false stories
Sneaking	Acting in a mean and secretive manner
Splendor	Brilliant appearance
Steadfast	Firm in belief or purpose
Steed	A riding horse
Stratagem	A plan, action or strategy
Succor	Help
Sūrah	Chapter of the Qur'ān
Sustain	To support

Suwar	Chapters of the Qur'ān, plural of Sūrah
Swarms	Large number of birds or people
Symbolize	To represent by using something as a symbol
Tawbah	Repentance, asking for forgiveness
Tawḥīd	Oneness of Allāh, Affirmation: There is no god but Allāh
Thamūd	A nation in ancient world, destroyed by Allāh for its disobedience
Theme	A subject or topic
Thorny	Painful
Tidings	News
Transliterate	To change letters or words in one language into corresponding letters or words of another language according to its original pronunciation
Treacherous	Dangerous, unreliable
Treaties	Agreements, understandings
Triumphant	Victorious, successful
Ultimate	Final
'Ummah	Nation
'Ummu-l-Kitāb	Mother of the Book, name of *Sūrah Al-Fātiḥah* in the Qur'ān
Vendor	A person who sells
Vicegerent	A deputy, one who is given powers to serve as a representative of chief
Waḥī	Revelation
Wandering	Moving from one place to another place
Whim	An odd idea
Whisperer	One who spreads gossips
Witchcraft	Magic practice
Woe	A grief, pain or curse
Worldly	earthly or materialistic thing connected to this world
Wrath	Anger
Wretched	Worthless, poor in condition
Yieldeth	Gives
Zakāh	Islamic tax, a charity

Appendix II

THE SIGN OF THE 'ĀYAH

Every language has its signs of writing, the punctuation marks, to guide the reader through various parts of the speech. Without punctuation marks it is often difficult to make exact sense. In English we use the signs of ,.;:'"? to help proper reading.

Punctuation marks are more important in Arabic; it is the language of the Revelation and must be read and understood exactly as it was revealed, recited and understood by Rasūlullāh (S) and his *Ṣaḥābah* (R). Arabic writing was in its initial stage when the Qur'ān was revealed. Muslims not only developed an elaborate system of writing to preserve the exact pronunciation of Arabic text, they also preserved systems of reading for preserving the ways in which the Qur'ān was recited by Rasūlullāh (S) and his *Ṣaḥābah.*

The Qur'ānic Arabic *'Āyah*, a circular sign (o), is used to indicate various types of pauses or stops. There are further letter signs placed on the *'Āyah* (or in *'Āyah)* to indicate what kind of stop that is. There are also other signs in the Qur'ān to help read each verse properly. The best way to learn the Qur'ān is through a teacher; a well prepared text and audio and videos could also help a great deal. All *'Āyah* signs and other signs must be learned properly and followed carefully in reading the Qur'ān. To facilitate reading the *Transliteration* in the *Juz'* we have used end of the *'Āyāt* as *al-waqf al-muṭlaq* (absolute stop), even when we had the option to continue. In Arabic regular ending of the last word often changes before *'Āyah.* Some *ḥarakāt* are replaced and some letters are interchanged. In this **textbook** we have placed the silent *ḥarakah* or *ḥarakāt* inside brackets and new letter which replaces *ḥarakāt* (in case it happens) is added before the bracket, in **bold**. Once a reader learns the proper recitation he / she can go with the options.

Here are the signs:

O : sign of an *'Āyah* (آيَة), follow the sign on it; if no sign then stop.

ط : ***Al-Waqf al-Muṭlaq*** (اَلْوَقْفُ الْمُطْلَق), Absolute Stop; stop is compulsory, the subject continues.

م : ***Al-Waqf al-Lāzim*** (اَلْوَقْفُ اللاَّزِم), Compulsory Stop; no stopping changes the meaning.

ج : ***Al-Waqf al-Jā'iz*** (اَلْوَقْفُ الْجَائِز), Permissible Stop; better to stop, to continue is allowed.

لا : ***Lā*** (لا), No; stop is optional, does not affect the meaning.

ز : ***Al-Waqf al-Mujawwaz***(اَلْوَقْف الْمُجَوَّز), Permitted Stop; permitted to stop, better to continue.

صلى : *Al-Waqf al-Murakhkhas*, (اَلْوَقْفُ الْمُرَخَّصُ), preferable to continue; stopping is permitted.

صلے : *Al-Wasl al-Awlā*, (اَلْوَصْلُ الأَوْلَى), Preferred Connection; preferable to continue.

ق : *Qīla 'alaihi al-Waqf* (قِيلَ عَلَيْهِ الْوَقْفُ), Stop Obligatory; must stop.

صل : *Qad Yūsal* (قَدْ يُوصَلُ), both stop or continuation permitted.

قف : *Qif* (قِفْ), Stop; a complete stop ordered.

لا : *Lā* (لاَ), No; no stop when inside the text.

ك : *Kadhālika*, (كَذَلِكَ), Same as Before; previous sign must be followed.

وقفة : *Waqfah* (وَقْفَةٌ), Long Breath; take a long breath then continue without stopping.

س سكتة : *Saktah* (سَكْتَةٌ), Short Breath; take a small breath then continue without break.

IQRA'
ARABIC TRANSLITERATION CHART

q	ق	*	z	ز		'	أء	*
k	ك		s	س		b	ب	
l	ل		sh	ش		t	ت	
m	م		s	ص	*	th	ث	*
n	ن		d	ض	*	j	ج	
h	هـ		t	ط	*	h	ح	*
w	و		z	ظ	*	kh	خ	*
y	ي		'	ع	*	d	د	
			gh	غ	*	dh	ذ	*
			f	ف		r	ر	

SHORT VOWELS	LONG VOWELS	DIPHTHONGS
a \ ـَ	ā \ ـَا	aw \ ـَوْ
u \ ـُ	ū \ ـُو	ai \ ـَيْ
i \ ـِ	ī \ ـِي	

Such as: *kataba* كَتَبَ Such as: *Kitāb* كِتَاب Such as: *Lawḥ* لَوْح

Such as: *Qul* قُلْ Such as: *Mamnūn* مَمْنُون Such as: *'Ain* عَيْن

Such as: *Ni'mah* نِعْمَة Such as: *Dīn* دِين

* Special attention should be given to the symbols marked with stars for they have no equivalent in the English sounds .

*** *Special Note on the Transliteration of Words Involving the Definite Article* (ال)**

- There are situations where the 'alif (ا) of the Definite Article is not pronounced though it is present in writing. To account for this type of 'Alif in the transliteration system, we have added an (a) in parenthesis before the Lam.(ال)

Example :

Al-Ḥamdu li Allāhi Rabbi al-'Ālamīn, is written as
Al-Ḥamdu li-(A)llāhi Rabbi (a)l-Ālamīn, and read as
Al-Ḥamdu li-llāhi Rabbi-l-'Ālamīn

ISLAMIC INVOCATIONS:

Rasūlullāh, *Ṣalla Allahu 'alaihi wa Sallam* (صَلَّى ٱللَّهُ عَلَيْهِ وَسَلَّم), and the Qur'ān teach us to glorify Allah (SWT) when we mention His Name and to invoke His Blessings when we mention the names of His Angels, Messengers, the *Ṣaḥābah* and the Pious Ancestors.

When we mention the Name of Allah we must say: *Subḥāna-hu Wa-Ta'ālā* (سُبْحَانَهُ وَتَعَالَى), Glorified is He and High. In this book we write (SWT) to remind us to Glorify Allah.

When we mention the name of Rasūlullāh (S) we must say: *Ṣalla Allāhu 'alai-hi wa-Sallam,* (صَلَّى ٱللَّهُ عَلَيْهِ وَسَلَّم), May Allah's Blessings and Peace be upon him.
We write an (Ṣ) to remind us to invoke Allah's Blessings on Rasūlullāh.

When we mention the name of an angel or a prophet we must say: *Alai-hi-s-Salām* (عَلَيْهِ ٱلسَّلاَم), Upon him be peace.
We write an (A) to remind us to invole Allah's Peace upon him.

When we hear the name of the *Ṣaḥābah* we must say:
For more than two, *Raḍiy-Allāhu Ta'ālā 'anhum,* (رَضِيَ ٱللَّهُ تَعَالَى عَنْهُم), May Allah be pleased with them.
For two of them, *Raḍiy-Allāhu Ta'ālā 'an-humā* (رَضِيَ ٱللَّهُ تَعَالَى عَنْهُمَا), May Allah be pleased with both of them.
For a *Ṣaḥābī*, *Raḍiy-Allāhu Ta'ālā 'an-hu* (رَضِيَ ٱللَّهُ تَعَالَى عَنْهُ), May Allah be pleased with him.
For a *Ṣaḥābiyyah*, *Raḍiy-Allāhu Ta'ālā 'an-hā* (رَضِيَ ٱللَّهُ تَعَالَى عَنْهَا), May Allah be pleased with her.
We write (R) to remind us to invoke Allah's Pleasure with a *Ṣaḥābī* or with *Ṣaḥābah.*

When we hear the name of the Pious Ancestor *(As-Salaf as-Ṣāliḥ)* we must say.
For a man, *Raḥmatullāh 'alaihi* (رَحْمَةُ ٱللَّهِ عَلَيْهِ), May Allah's Mercy be upon him.
For a woman, *Raḥmatullāh 'alai-hā* (رَحْمَةُ ٱللَّهِ عَلَيْهَا), May Allah's Mercy be with her.

ABOUT THIS TEXTBOOK

IQRA' International is pleased to offer two textbooks (with accompanying workbooks) specially prepared for the classrooms and for organized study (both individual and group) at the junior level: *Juz' 'Amma: 30, Volume 1* (From *An-Nās:114* to *Ash-Shams: 89* with *Sūrah Al-Fātiḥah:1)* and *Juz' 'Amma:30, Volume 2* (From *Al-Balad:90* to *An-Naba' :78)*. The adults will find these textbooks equally useful.

Most of the *Suwar* in the last *Juz'* (30) are Makkan and deal with the theme of *Tawḥīd* (The Oneness of Allāh), The *Risālah* (Prophethood), *Al-'Ākhirah,* (the Hereafter), and basic Islamic moral and ethical virtues. These condemn the *Kufr* (disbelief), the *shirk* (any assocation with Allah) and immoral behavior.

Each textbook is divided into systematic lessons with each lesson containing *an Introduction, Arabic text, two translations* ('Abdullāh Yūsuf 'Ali and M. M. Pickthall), *explanation, "We Have Learned," and a complete vocabulary of Arabic text* and a detailed *Glossary* of difficult words. Three appendices explain *The Signs of the Āyah, Arabic transliteration and Islamic invocations.* A detailed introduction provides important guidance for the teachers.

Abidullah Ghazi, M. A. Political Science (Alig), M. Sc. Econ. (LSE, London), Ph. D. Comparative Religions (Harvard)

Dr. Abidullah Ghazi, Executive Director of IQRA' International Educational Foundation, and his wife, Dr. Tasneema Ghazi, Director of Curriculum, are co-founders of IQRA' International Educational Foundation (a non-profit Islamic educational trust) and Chief Editors of its Educational Program. They have combined their talents and expertise and dedicated their lives to produce a Comprehensive Program of Islamic Studies for our children and youth and to develop IQRA' into a major center of research and development for Islamic Studies, specializing in Islamic education.

Dr. Abidullah Ghazi, a specialist in Islamic Studies and Comparative Religion, belongs to a prominent family of the Ulama' of India. His family has been active in the field of Islamic education, *da wah*, and struggle for freedom. Dr. Ghazi's early education was carried in traditional *Madaris*. He has studied at Muslim University, Aligarh, The London School of Economics, and Harvard University. He has taught at the Universities of Jamia Millia Islamia, Delhi, London, Harvard, San Diego, Minnesota, Northwestern, Governors State and King Abdul Aziz University, Jeddah. He is a consultant for the development of the program of Islamic Studies in various schools and universities. He is a well–known community worker, speaker, writer and poet.